YOUR LIFE
IN
GOD

YOUR LIFE
IN
GOD

By

Lucy McKee

Your Life in God
ISBN: 978-0-88144-154-3
Copyright © 2010 by Lucy McKee

Published by
Thorncrown Publishing
A Division of Yorkshire Publishing Group
9731 East 54th Street
Tulsa, OK 74146
www.thorncrownpublishing.com

Contents

Contents

Contents

HOW TO WALK WITH GOD AND FULFILL YOUR DESTINY 139

HOW TO SEEK GOD AND FIND ANSWERS

Introduction

In the presence of the Lord is fullness of joy (Ps. 16:11). In the presence of the Lord, there is everything we need — everything that pertains to the godly fulfillment of our lives here on earth. In God's presence are also answers and impartations to help prepare us for our divine purpose and call. When we enter His presence, God can transfer more and more of Himself into our hearts to help us fulfill all He has called us to do.

Life as God designed it and divine impartations don't fall on us by chance, and they are not automatically given simply because we accept Jesus into our hearts. We are told in the New Testament that when we ask, it will be given; when we seek, we will find; and when we knock, the door will be opened unto us (Luke 11:9). This lets us know that *we* have a part to play in making sure that God's purposes come to pass in our lives. We must *ask*, we must *seek*, and we must *knock*.

Many times, however, we don't understand the importance of asking, seeking, and knocking, nor do we know how to act on these divine commands. In this book, we will explore what it really means to seek the Lord in every situation of life. We can receive from Him *whatever* we need — but we must first learn to *ask*, *seek*, and *knock* according to the pattern God sets forth in His Word.

Lucy McKee

3

CHAPTER I

Break Up Your Fallow Ground

God calls us to seek Him, but that divine call comes with instructions to follow and prerequisites to fulfill. Hosea 10:12 (*AMP*) gives us insight into *when* and *how* we are to seek the Lord.

> **Sow for yourselves according to righteousness (uprightness and right standing with God); reap according to mercy and loving-kindness. Break up your uncultivated ground, for it is time to seek the Lord, to inquire for and of Him, and to require His favor, till He comes and teaches you righteousness and rains His righteous gift of salvation upon you.**

We can know it is time to diligently seek the Lord when:

1. We're not satisfied with where we are in our spiritual walk.
2. We know the circumstances that surround us need to change.

It is in these times that God commands us *to break up our fallow ground*. This is not something He will do for us. It is *our* responsibility to break up the fallow ground in our own hearts.

Preparing the Ground of Your Heart

Fallow ground is ground left untended. It is ground that is dry and cracked. The soil has not been tilled, and no seed has been sown. Ground in this kind of poor condition results either from neglect or from bad weather, such as a long drought.

Have you ever had "bad weather" in your life — times of affliction, persecution, pressure, or spiritual drought? These kinds of challenges can cause the ground of your heart to become dry and hard. But in seasons of adversity, you need to do the same thing a farmer does to his fallow ground before planting seed. He uses a plow to break up the hard surface of the soil, turning it over so that softer, moister soil is on top. Then he waters and cultivates the ground until it is ready for seed to be sown in it.

In the same way, we will each have times in our lives when God calls us to break up the dry, hard, fallow ground of our hearts until we are once more ready to receive the seed of His Word. During these times, God lets us know that the time is *now* to seek Him and to yield to His Spirit's work to bring needed change in certain areas of our lives.

An Ongoing Process
Until the Answer Comes

In the case of the prophet Hosea, the people to whom he prophesied needed to attain right standing with God. Therefore, Hosea told them by the word of the Lord that it was time for them to seek the Lord for their salvation.

Also, we see here that seeking God is not a one-time prayer. It is a posture of pursuing God in prayer until our answer comes. We are to seek God until He intervenes in our situation to save us — regardless of what it is that we need to be saved *from*.

The key to understanding this process is that our salvation does not manifest until *He comes* and *it rains*.

> **...His going forth is prepared and certain as the dawn and He will come to us as the (heavy) rain, as the latter rain that waters the earth.**
>
> **Hosea 6:3 *AMP***

The rain that is spoken of is Jesus Himself. His going forth to manifest our answer is prepared, and it is as certain as the dawn.

How certain are we that morning will come each day? We have no doubt. In the same way, Jesus will come to us as the rain. He doesn't come just as the Savior, the Healer, or the Redeemer; He comes to us as the rain, pouring down upon us whatever it is we need at any given moment.

Jesus Our Savior
In Every Situation of Life

Hosea tells us to seek Jesus until He comes as our Savior. Even though we may have already prayed the initial prayer of salvation, we still need Jesus to be our Savior each day in every circumstance that life brings to us.

Jesus' role in our lives is specifically to save us. So when we're not satisfied with the way things are, it is time to seek the Lord until He comes to save us. In that act of saving, He gives us understanding. He gives us healing. He sets us free. He delivers and brings provision to us. However, it is up to us to seek Him until those blessings manifest in our lives.

In the following chapters, we will look at some other scriptures that refer to seeking the Lord. I believe you will gain more understanding about what it means to seek the Lord and how it is done. This is such an important subject for you to understand, for it is a key in defining how you are to live your life before God.

CHAPTER 2

Answer God
With His Word

God doesn't require us to be tremendously spiritual people before we can come to Him. We're not required to have our act together and to be nearly perfect in all we say or do in order to seek His face. No, the Bible says that when we draw near to God, we must simply *believe that He is*.

> **But without faith it is impossible to please and be satisfactory to Him. For whoever would come near to God must believe that God exists and that He is the rewarder of those who earnestly and diligently seek Him.**
>
> **Hebrews 11:6** *AMP*

In the first part of this verse, we see that all we must have in order to come to God is *faith*. Faith simply believes that God *is*.

A Good Place to Start
In Seeking God

There are times when I come to God believing I know something about the situation I'm facing. In those times, I might pray something like this: *"Father, I don't know everything there is to know about this situation, but I do know this part and I am positive that this other part is true."*

Then as I sit under the weight of God's presence, I begin to realize that I'm not really 100-percent sure about one of those "facts" I thought I knew for certain, so I scratch that point out of my prayer. As my conversation with the Lord progresses, I keep backing up on the "facts" I think I know. Finally, I often reach the place where I realize all I *really* know is that *He is God.*

That is actually a very good place to start in our seeking of the Lord. He asks us to draw near to Him, believing that He is God.

What It Means
To Diligently Seek the Lord

Second, if we are going to draw near to God, we must believe that He rewards those who diligently seek Him.

Some people have gotten the wrong impression about this phrase "diligently seek," and they misunderstand what it actually means. It *doesn't* mean God expects His children to stay on bowed knees and pray in one place all day long. That isn't realistic.

Most of us don't have the ability to spend the bulk of every day waiting before the Lord like that. Nevertheless, we *can* live our lives moment by moment *for* Him as we keep our hearts open *before* Him.

To diligently seek the Lord also doesn't mean that we must always speak to God loudly or fervently. It simply means that we speak to God from our hearts. *Thus, the secret to seeking God is to learn how to pour out to the Lord in prayer what is inside our own hearts.*

A Mother Who Poured Out Her Heart
Before the Lord

We see an example of this in First Samuel 1, when Hannah went to the tabernacle of the Lord to pray earnestly for a child.

So Hannah rose after they had eaten and drunk in Shiloh. Now Eli the priest was sitting on his seat beside a post of the temple (tent) of

the Lord. And [Hannah] was in distress of soul, praying to the Lord and weeping bitterly.

She vowed, saying, O Lord of hosts, if You will indeed look on the affliction of Your handmaid and [earnestly] remember, and not forget Your handmaid but will give me a son, I will give him to the Lord all his life; no razor shall touch his head.

And as she continued praying before the Lord, Eli noticed her mouth. Hannah was speaking in her heart; only her lips moved but her voice was not heard. So Eli thought she was drunk.

Eli said to her, How long will you be intoxicated? Put wine away from you.

But Hannah answered, No, my lord, I am a woman of a sorrowful spirit. I have drunk neither wine nor strong drink, but I WAS POURING OUT MY SOUL BEFORE THE LORD.

1 Samuel 1:9-15 *AMP*

Hannah was praying from her heart. Although Eli the priest couldn't hear any sounds, he noticed Hannah's lips moving. She was pouring out all that was in her heart unto the Lord.

You might think you don't have anything in your heart to pour out before the Lord. But you'd be surprised to learn how much has been pushed down and buried in your heart over the years. Whether those inner thoughts that lie hidden inside you are right or wrong, God's call to you is the same: "Pour out everything in your heart to Me. Speak it all out to Me in prayer." This is a crucial first step in seeking Him.

Don't Answer Yourself With Your Own Thoughts

Colossians 3:3 says that *all* of your life is hidden in Christ in God. Therefore, the best place to find out about yourself and about what you are supposed to do in life is in His presence. Come to God and seek Him diligently.

Once again, seeking God diligently doesn't mean to pray loudly or for hours at a time. It means to seek Him with your whole heart. You are to come into His presence by faith and pour out all that is in your heart.

One mistake to avoid after you pour out the thoughts of your heart to the Lord is to then try to answer yourself with more of your own thoughts. An example might sound something like this: *"I've been thinking about this matter that's been on my heart, Lord. I think I should deal with it in one of two ways. If So-and-so responds this way, I'll say this. Then if that doesn't work, I'll try this."*

You will never walk in God's wisdom for your life if you resort to that kind of praying. There's a better way to approach the Lord after pouring out your heart in prayer. Just say, *"Father, I've told You what is on my heart. Now this is what Your Word says about it."*

After giving the Lord all that is in your heart, speak out what you know He says in His Word about those matters. *Answer the cry of your heart with God's Word.* Seek Him with His Word. Take the Word of God with you as you draw near to Him, and then speak that Word to Him in prayer.

I want to share some examples to show you the way this kind of prayer might sound in various situations.

- *"Father, even though it seems so dry in my life right now — even though I feel like Your presence is no longer near — I know that Your Word says You will NEVER leave me or forsake me* [Heb. 13:5].*"*
- *"Lord, I have this dream in my heart, but I don't know which way to go. However, I thank You for Your Word that says my steps are ordered of the Lord* [Ps. 37:23]. *Thank You for Your promise that my feet will never be caught in a net as I follow Your will for my life* [Ps. 25:15].*"*
- *"Lord, I don't know what course in life You have planned for me to take. But I trust Your Word, which says that You who have started a good work in me will complete it until the day of Christ Jesus* [Phil. 1:6].*"*

This is the way we are to seek God with His own Word. First, we must look in the Word to find scriptures that deal with the problems we are facing in our lives. Then we take those specific scriptures with us as we come before the Lord to pour out our hearts to Him in prayer.

Hold Fast to the Lifeline
Of God's Word

As you seek God and wait before Him in this way, His Word establishes you and keeps your soul steady in the storm. It becomes a part of you, causing you to rise above the circumstances you face.

The truth of God's Word will act like a lifeline when you feel like you're drowning in the circumstances that surround you. As you speak God's promises into your situation, that lifeline will keep pulling you *into* God and the answer you are looking for as it pulls you *away from* the problems you're struggling to overcome.

If you were literally drowning and someone threw you a lifeline, you certainly wouldn't refuse that offer of help. In the same way, you must take heed to the wisdom God has already given you in His Word.

Draw near to God by faith, knowing that He is God. In that position of simple trust, begin to lift up to Him those matters that weigh heavily in your heart. Pour out your heart before God with the confident expectation that He *will* answer you.

God will throw you the lifeline of His Word to hold you steady when the waves of circumstances are crashing over you. And as you diligently answer your own prayers with the words He has given you, that lifeline of truth will pull you into the answer you require so you can walk out His will in every situation.

CHAPTER 3

Seed to Sow
And Bread to Eat

No matter what we are dealing with in life, we can know that God's thoughts are always higher than our thoughts about the situation. God confirms this in Isaiah 55:

> Seek, inquire for, and require the Lord while he may be found (claiming Him by necessity and by right); call upon Him while he is near....
>
> For My thoughts are not your thoughts, neither are your ways My ways, says the Lord. FOR AS THE HEAVENS ARE HIGHER THAN THE EARTH, SO ARE MY WAYS HIGHER THAN YOUR WAYS AND MY THOUGHTS THAN YOUR THOUGHTS.
>
> For as the rain and snow come down from the heavens, and return not there again, but water the earth and make it bring forth and sprout, that it may give SEED TO THE SOWER AND BREAD TO THE EATER, SO SHALL MY WORD BE that goes forth out of My mouth; it shall not return to Me void (without producing any effect, useless), but it shall accomplish that which I please and purpose, and it shall prosper in the thing for which I sent it.

Isaiah 55:6,8-11 *AMP*

We're going to keep building on what we've already discussed as we look at this passage of Scripture. There is much truth contained in these verses, but we'll focus on the excellent description we find here of how we are to seek God.

The Divine Exchange

One of the first things we see in this passage is that our thoughts are not God's thoughts, nor are our ways His ways. His thoughts are higher, and our thoughts are lower. His ways are higher, and our ways are lower. As soon as we know God's higher thoughts regarding a given situation, we can begin to walk in His higher ways. But for this to happen, our thoughts and our ways must *change*.

What is the most effective way to transform our thoughts and our ways? We must give God our lower thoughts and exchange them for His higher thoughts. His thoughts have an elevating effect on our minds and character. When His thoughts come to us, they automatically make us rise to take our rightful place, seated in heavenly places in Christ (Eph. 2:6). From that lofty vantage point, we can put all the problems and challenges we face in proper perspective. Outside pressure may try to bombard our minds and emotions, but *nothing* can keep us down as long as God's higher thoughts are dominant in our hearts.

The passage we just read likens the rain and the snow that fall from the sky to God's thoughts. These verses paint a picture of the divine exchange that occurs as we seek God: Our thoughts go up in prayer, and His thoughts come down to us to bring revelation to our hearts.

God's Higher Thoughts
As
Both *Seed* and *Bread*

This exchange of our lower thoughts for God's higher thoughts provides *seed to the sower*. We don't eat seeds — we *sow* them. This exchange also gives *bread to the eater*. We don't plant bread — we *eat* it.

You don't eat seed, nor do you plant bread. And according to the Bible, this natural principle also applies to God's words in the spiritual realm. Sometimes His words will be seed for you to sow back to Him in prayer. Sometimes His words will be given back to you as bread to eat — substance with which to feed your spirit and give you direction as you walk out His will in a given situation.

God has placed within our hearts both the *seed* and the *bread* of God's Word. But how do we know when to *plant* the Word by speaking it forth in prayer? And when is the Word *bread* to us? In other words, when is God's Word something we've received from Him as necessary sustenance to walk out a particular journey of faith in our lives?

When we pray, we pour out the thoughts of our hearts to the Lord about situations we're facing, about our divine call, about His plans for us and for others, and so forth. Then God responds back to our hearts with His higher thoughts.

Here's how we can determine if we've just received *seed* or *bread* from the Father's hand:

- If we still don't have enough information to enable us to walk out of the problem we're facing or to move into the plan God has for our lives, then His words to us in our hearts are *seed*. What do we do with seed? We sow it up in prayer. We speak back to God what He has already given *us*.
- With all the information we have in our hearts, if we still don't know where to place our feet or which way to walk, that information is *seed.*
- If we don't yet have enough information from God to carry out what He wants us to do in a given situation, the facts we've received thus far are *seed.*
- If the words of God concerning the matter we've lifted up in prayer are not yet a solid foundation underneath our feet that enables us to make it to the other side, those words are *seed.*
- But what if we *have* received enough information to step out in faith and find victory in a situation we're facing, in the circumstances we're facing, or in relation to our call? In that

17

case, God's higher thoughts to us are _bread_ to strengthen and sustain us until we have successfully made it through the challenge we are facing.

What to Do with Heaven's Seed

What do you do with seed? You _plant_ it by speaking the Word you have received from the Father. Sow that seed by sending it back up to the Father in prayer. Tell Him, _"Father, this is my highest thought at this time. Here is what I have in my heart about this matter that I believe I heard from You."_

Plant your seed. Tell God again what is in your heart. Ask Him to show you which part of your thoughts is of Him and which is not.

You see, not all of your thoughts come from your soul. As you pour out your heart about a certain matter, some of the thoughts you share with the Lord might very well be seed that He has already planted in your heart. However, God wants to keep adding to that seed until His words have become bread to eat and to sustain your spirit as you walk through that situation.

That's why you must plant the seed God has already given you. Sow that seed by speaking out in faith what He has already spoken to your heart regarding that particular subject.

The Purifying Process
Of Seeking God

If the thoughts you pour out to the Lord in prayer are not right — if they don't bring truth and light to the situation — God won't send those thoughts back down to your heart again as you continue to pray. Instead, He will exchange your lower thoughts for His _higher_ thoughts.

So the next time you seek God about a particular situation, don't stop after pouring out your heart before Him. Make sure you're prepared to receive something back from _Him_. Remember, seeking God is a dialogue, _not_ a monologue. The Lord will rain His higher thoughts into your heart; then He expects you to return those thoughts back to Him by speaking them out in faith as you pray.

Each time you go through this process of divine exchange, God will cleanse and purify your thoughts a little more. He will take away that which is not of Him and plant back into your heart every thought that *is* of Him. Those higher thoughts from Heaven will then act as living seed that one day produces bread for you to eat — all the way through that situation until you make it safely to the other side.

CHAPTER 4

Becoming Like-Minded With God

When God imparts the seed of His life-giving truth to your spirit, you are not meant to carry that seed in your heart without giving it back to Him. Every seed dropped into your heart from Heaven was given to you for the purpose of sowing it again.

So if you don't know enough about what to do in a given situation, don't add your own thoughts to the wisdom He has given you. Just plant the seed you've received by speaking it out in prayer back to the Lord.

"Father God, this is what I have in my heart about this situation. I have accumulated all these thoughts concerning the matter, and I am now giving them all back to You."

Does God already know those things you are sharing with Him? Yes, He does — but He's trying to teach you how to *ask*, *seek*, and *knock*. He wants you to learn how to walk *with* Him through every situation of life. This is training ground for you to become all that God has created you to become.

If You Are 'Otherwise-Minded'

In my times of prayer, I surrender to God the thoughts of my heart and then ask Him to help me see those matters as He sees them. For instance, I may say something like this to the Lord:

"Father, something is in my heart concerning this line of ministry. Am I thinking wrongly about it? According to Philippians 3:15, I know that if in any respect I have a different attitude of mind than You do on this matter, You will make that clear to me. So please show me the right way to think about this, Father."

If you are "otherwise-minded" about any subject you are praying about, God will let you know. That is His responsibility. He will reveal the thoughts in your heart that are contrary to His higher thoughts.

Sometimes we receive only a part of God's plan for our lives. Many times He shows us one thing to do, and we add twelve more items to the original assignment that are *not* in His plan for us. We may have a zeal for God and we may want to obey Him. But if we let our minds wander from what we know He has told us, we can easily begin to add to His instructions using our own natural reasoning.

It's amazing how many natural thoughts can run through our minds, bringing new ideas of things for us to do. But if we act on those thoughts, they can distract us and hinder our ability to fulfill God's will for our lives.

That's why we must continually give the Lord access to our hearts, in prayer, so He can cleanse our innermost thoughts and reveal to us what is of Him and what is not. Then we must continue to seek God to find out *how* He wants us to fulfill what is in our hearts from Him. Certainly we can't bring His plan to pass on our own. We need to know His *higher ways*.

His Plan Is the Only Plan That Works

In the Old Testament, we see that the nation of Israel was definitely supposed to conquer Jericho (*see* Joshua chapter 6). But there was a right way — a *higher* way — to do it, and it involved a plan that wasn't natural to man's mind. Both the plan and the power to *accomplish* that plan had to come from God Himself.

Likewise, God has revealed to *you* a portion of His good plan for your life. However, you must remain in an ongoing dialogue with Him so you can perfect your understanding of that divine plan. You can't stop until you know not only what you are called to do, but also *how* and *when* you are to do it.

The key to your success is your knowledge of the exact steps to take and the correct timing in which to take them. But you can only receive that wisdom as you continually wait before God in His presence and speak His Word to Him in prayer. Only your obedience to *His* plans and your dependence on *His* power will bring it all to pass.

You may go to the Father in prayer with what you *think* is bread you've received from Him. You may even be ready to step out and act on that "bread" — when all of a sudden the Holy Spirit alerts you that most of your plan is a product of *your* thoughts, not His.

The Holy Spirit may speak to your heart, saying, *"I did tell you to do these three things — but I did NOT tell you to do this other thing that you have on your agenda. Don't do it."* Then the Lord may continue to whittle down your thoughts on that other matter until you have nothing left but a little seed.

What do you do if a seed is all you're left with? *You plant that seed by giving it back to the Lord in prayer.* Then you spend time in God's presence, allowing Him to give back to you His higher thoughts and ways regarding those specific areas where you need more guidance and wisdom. This is how you learn to accurately seek God with all of your heart.

Seek God for Further Light
On the Matters That Matter Most

I've made a practice of this over the years of my walk with God. Countless times I've come into God's presence and poured out my heart to Him, seeking Him for more light on His plan for my life.

"Father, what about this issue that pertains to Your future plans for me? I've had something in my heart about this subject ever since I got saved."

"Lord, years I ago I heard You speak to my heart and tell me that I would go to the nations. What did You mean by that, Father? When will it occur? What needs to take place first?"

I sowed these thoughts in prayer up to the Father's throne. I didn't have any idea how the dreams He'd put in my heart would come to pass. I just knew that God had said He was going to send me to other nations with the revelations He had given me. The *how* and *where* and *when* came as I kept sowing in prayer the seed of His words that were already planted in my heart. Then further revelation came, and that seed became bread for me to walk out on.

Seeking God
In the Realm of Relationships

Many times people are waiting for supernatural breakthroughs to occur in their lives that will take them to the next level in His plans for them. The problem is, that those same people haven't given God anything to work with. They haven't spent time in His presence, seeking Him in prayer until the seed of His Word planted in their hearts becomes the bread that they must have to walk out His plan.

This same principle applies to our relationships. We would have so much more harmony in our relationships with others if we'd learn to take everything to the Lord when an issue arises before we tried to "talk things through" with that person according to our own lower thoughts and ways.

"Lord, the other night my son came home and made this disturbing statement. What he said really bothered me, Father, and I wanted to let him have it! But I decided I need to know what YOU think about it before I say anything to him."

Too often we miss it by trying to handle situations according to our own thoughts and our own ways. But our thoughts and ways are so much lower than *God's* thoughts and ways.

Don't try to deal with relationship issues according to your own reasoning. Pour out your heart to the Lord about those issues, and allow Him to give you the wisdom you need.

"I don't know about You, Lord, but I personally thought what my son said stunk! What do You think? What would You have me say and do?"

If we will only take the time to seek God for *His* wisdom on how to deal with the situation, we will experience a better outcome every time.

Learning to live like this will keep us from becoming "nags" in our own homes. Too often we try to produce needed change in our relationships in our own strength. But every time we deal with these issues out of our own minds, we are sowing only into this lower, natural realm.

On the other hand, we'll experience an entirely different outcome if we will act according to God's higher ways. Whenever we face a difficult situation in one of our relationships, we should pour out our hearts to the Lord about the matter before we ever speak what's on our mind to the other person. Then we must wait before God until we receive His wisdom on how to proceed. Every time we seek the Lord in this way, we sow into His higher realm of the Spirit — the realm where all our answers reside.

When you're in the midst of a difficult situation with another person and you yield the matter to God, you give Him the opportunity to either change your mind or the mind of the person you're talking to Him about. This is all part of having faith in God. You will receive an answer for every situation as you rest in His ability to cleanse and purify every single area of your life.

"Father, these are my thoughts about this situation. But if I'm not thinking the way that YOU are thinking about this matter, I'm asking You to let me know."

God will never move unless we give Him seed to work with. Most relationship issues get stuck in our hearts, and our thoughts just keep going around and around the same track. We have a thought about the situation, and then we answer that thought with another of our own thoughts. As a result, we never receive *God's* answer for the situation — which is the only answer that leads to peace and a victorious resolution.

Sometimes the thoughts that circle around and around in our minds about a problem we're having with someone else are actually from the devil. The Lord will help us see our thoughts for what they are so we can acknowledge their source. But we still need to plant those thoughts in prayer. Then God is obligated to send back to us seed that is clean and pure.

"Father, I know that what I've been thinking regarding this relationship is of the devil. Please give me Your thoughts about the matter so I can begin to see that person and this situation the way YOU see it."

James 5:16 (*AMP*) tells you that your *earnest, heartfelt prayer makes tremendous power available, dynamic in its working.* Even if you know that the thoughts you have to offer up in prayer are "otherwise-minded" regarding a situation you're dealing with, you can still activate God's power with your simple prayer of faith. As you lift up the thoughts of your heart to Him, He will then give back His higher thoughts — seed from His Word that will become the power you need to act out what He has shown you.

Reaching Our God-Ordained Destination

God is wonderful at "unraveling the tangles" in our lives and keeping us from getting out of His will as we seek Him. My own life has often looked like an utter mystery to me. I know there is no way I could have conceived in my own mind the course my life has taken, nor could I have ever found the natural power to get myself where I am now in ministry. It has all been of the Lord's making. All I did was make it a practice to seek Him on a daily basis.

At one time or another, all of us have conceived of plans that were of our own making. But our lower thoughts and ways will never take us to the destination God has ordained for us. It is only *His* plans for our lives that will be established. This is the reason this message is so crucial, for we will only become prepared for our divine purpose and call as we determine to diligently seek God every day of our lives.

CHAPTER 5

Seek the Lord
In Every Situation of Life

If we go through life sowing only to this natural realm that we see, we won't allow the Father's good and perfect will to work in our lives. But when we learn to sow everything in our hearts to God in prayer, we can then reap the blessing of His supernatural guidance and direction.

God is a good God, and He can work out situations that look impossible to us. When we yield to His plan in every area of our lives, He has the provisions to cause the answer we need to come to pass.

No Need Too Small For God

Understand this: There is *no* matter in our lives too small for God's ears.

For instance, one day when I was taking my elderly mother to a doctor's appointment, she was in urgent need of a restroom. So I prayed, *"Father, I thank You for a parking space that is close to the hospital entrance."*

Mom remarked that God was probably too busy to be concerned with our parking space in front of the hospital. But I prayed again, *"Father, You said everything that concerns me concerns You [Ps. 138:8]. And right now, I am greatly concerned about my mother and the convenient parking space we need. I can't carry her in, and I know she has to use the restroom quickly, so my highest thought right now is our need to hurry."*

The Lord was right on time with His answer, providing the perfect parking space we needed at that moment.

This is the way to live life every moment of every day. We are to lift up every situation and need in our lives to the Lord in prayer. Then we are to receive back from Heaven God's higher thoughts and ways so we can walk in them.

Releasing the Concerns
Of Our Hearts in Prayer

Our hearts have different areas or compartments reserved for different things in our lives. Family, ministry, jobs, and friends each occupy different areas in our hearts.

Some things, such as a certain tribe in a foreign land, may occupy a very small place in your heart unless you are actually called to that particular mission field. You may only have a few thoughts concerning that specific tribe. Nevertheless, you are to lift up the thoughts you have about that tribe to the Lord in prayer. He may enlarge that place in your heart as you pray, or He may be satisfied with the seed you have planted in prayer for that particular need.

Our families usually occupy a large compartment in our hearts. In this compartment, we may have the needs of several children, a backslidden or an unsaved spouse, and the prospect of extended family coming to stay for a long visit. The compartment that contains concerns for our family members can get bigger and bigger in our hearts if we don't release those concerns to the Lord.

What is God going to do about it? If we don't seek Him for the answers we need, He will do *nothing*! That family compartment will just keep getting bigger and bigger in our hearts until we feel like exploding.

Now, we may go to God and say, *"I want to know why You haven't moved in this situation with my family. It's gotten out of hand!"*

But the Lord will reply, *"What seed have you planted in prayer? Why haven't you talked to Me about the situation and given Me something to work with?"*

Many times our problem is that we haven't acknowledged the seed of God's Word that resides within us. It's like going into a field and running farm machinery all day without ever planting any seed in the soil. It's possible to do that in life — to keep our motor running without ever planting one seed!

In other words, we can go through life trying to figure out everything with our own reasoning, never seeking the Lord to receive *His* wisdom regarding the situations we face. *But God is just waiting for us to pour out our hearts to Him so He can give us prayers to pray and words to say!*

In Conclusion

Let me stress again: God is calling you to break up the fallow ground of your heart, making it soft and ready to receive the seed of His Word. Then He wants you to seek Him with all that is in your heart.

So don't whine about your needs and concerns. Instead by faith lift up all that is in your heart to God. Stay in His presence long enough to allow Him to rain down on you the wisdom you need. That divine wisdom will water the ground of your heart, preparing you to receive God's words to you as seed. And as you continue to sow that seed back up to the Father in prayer, it won't be long before the seed becomes bread to sustain you as you walk out His will for your life.

If anyone can cause you to think right and to know God's higher thoughts and ways, it is your Heavenly Father. As you learn to continually fellowship with Him, giving Him access to every compartment of your heart, the Father will give you fresh revelation. He will teach you what it means to partake of His righteousness. He will show you the power that is at your disposal through the blood of His Son. You will no longer be ashamed in His presence, and each day you will come to know Him better.

This is the way you enter that place in the Spirit where the Father's wisdom resides where He can impart more and more of His heart into *your* heart to help you fulfill all He has called you to do.

This is the way you can live a life before God that bears *much* eternal fruit.

HOW TO JUST "BE" THERE BEFORE GOD

Introduction

We know from Scripture that "...faith comes by hearing, and hearing by the word of God." (Romans 10:17 NKJV) This hearing is really *hearing* and *hearing* and *hearing* the Word over and over again. It is hearing what the Holy Spirit and the Word of the Lord is saying to the Church so that we can grow and understand God more.

This truth is very important in my heart, and I believe the Lord really wants you to grasp this understanding. There are some messages concerning faith, the Holy Spirit, moves of God, and healing that you will hear over and over again. However, this message that I am about to share with you is probably something you will not hear with such earnest repetition.

Now, I'm not saying I have a message that the rest of the Body of Christ doesn't have. What I am saying is that the Lord wants you to understand that there are people in the Body of Christ that He entrusts different parts of Himself to, giving them a deeper understanding of His ways for a specific purpose. Therefore, I believe it is important that He illumine, or give light to, you in this area because of where you are going in Him.

God will always prepare you ahead of time for the different things He has planned and destined for your life. His preparation comes through the teaching of His Word and by the power of His Holy Spirit.

He has repeatedly brought this to me and underscored it in my heart for the purpose of passing it on to you. My prayer for you is that you have an encounter with Christ...

By having the eyes of your heart flooded with light, so that you can know and understand the hope to which He has called you, and how rich is His glorious inheritance in the saints (His set-apart ones).

Ephesians 1:18

CHAPTER 1

The Invitation

God said to Moses, Come up to the Lord, you and Aaron....

Exodus 24:1

God is omnipresent. In other words, His presence is everywhere. Not only is God everywhere, but He is also living *in* and *with* us in the person of the Holy Spirit (John 14:17). So, we really don't have to *go somewhere* to get into the presence of the Lord. Yet, all through the Word of God we see His invitation to "come up hither" or come to Him — just like He says to Moses here in Exodus 24. First Peter 2:4-5 is another example:

> *Come to Him* [then, to that] Living Stone which men tried and threw away, but which is chosen [and] precious in God's sight. [*Come*] and, like living stones, be yourselves built [into] a spiritual house, for a holy (dedicated, consecrated) priesthood, to offer up [those] spiritual sacrifices [that are] acceptable and pleasing to God through Jesus Christ.

Here, God says to come to Him, "the Living Stone," and be built into a *spiritual house*. Why are we to come to Him? He needs us to grow

35

and be built up in Him spiritually. First Peter 2:2, just two verses before, says, "As newborn babes, desire the pure milk of the word, that you may grow thereby (NKJV)."

Now you may think, *Well, I thought I could just read the Bible and get the sincere milk of the Word*. No. God says to those who desire the sincere milk of the Word to come to Him. We are not just to read the Word or pray the Word or confess the Word. We who desire the sincere milk of the Word, which is rich in spiritual nourishment and vitamins, must also come to Him. This is how we grow.

There are different times in our lives when we are at certain places, or levels of spiritual growth in Him, when we must accept His invitation and come to Him. The first time we came to Him was when we got saved. The truth is, anytime there is anything significant that happens in our walk with God, it will be because we come to Him.

Coming Is Continual

We also know that there is a *continual coming* to God, not just to a book. This enables us to really participate and interact with God and begin to learn who He is. Continually coming to Him also enables us to find out who we are in Him. All of our lives are hidden with Christ in God (Colossians 3:3). Therefore, to find out who we are, we must purposely come to Him. Yes, you can find out much about your identity in Him through the Word; but to be able to answer the specific things about you that are *not* in Scripture, you will have to come to Him.

When I was fifty years old, my family had been living in the same town for five generations; my husband's family for six generations. We never moved or even thought about moving, nor had I ever thought of going anywhere without my husband. I would go out and preach for three or four days at a time, and return home.

Then one day, the Lord spoke to me in my spirit and said, "You will be moving to a small town called Ozark, Alabama." He specifically told me that I would take a position there to train "pray-ers." Both my husband and I had a witness on this in our spirits and were in total agreement.

As we began to walk it out, we came to know with more and more certainty that everything about it lined up. In every way, the blessings of the Lord followed our decision. Although we still had many days that were challenging, we knew for sure that we had heard from God. If we had not been walking in the Spirit — walking in the assurance of what God had told us to do — we would have questioned whether what we were doing was right or not when the challenges came.

God had placed before us an opportunity, but it was not a specific opportunity that we could find in the Word. I could not look in the Bible and see that we were to move to the small town called Ozark, Alabama. Yet, because we had a habit of *continually coming to God*, we knew in our hearts He was leading us. As the result, we chose to participate *with Him*…and move.

CHAPTER 2

Going Deeper

In the Old Testament, we are given a wonderful example of how God leads, directs, and provides for His people. When He sent Moses to deliver the children of Israel from 400 years of slavery in Egypt, He manifested many miraculous signs and wonders for all to see. His demonstrations for them were truly magnificent.

We know that as they traveled through the desert, God led them with a cloud by day so that they would not be in the blistering heat, and a pillar of fire by night to keep them warm from the desert cold (Exodus 13:21). God took care of them using miracles; His powerful presence was with them and led them all the way to Mount Sinai. And yet, we see God say to Moses, Aaron, and the Israelites, "Come up to Me."

Just as He did with Moses, Aaron, and the nation of Israel, there will be times in your walk with God when you will hear a pronounced invitation in your heart to *come up to Him*. This is a strong feeling to leave where you are and what you are doing in order to come to Him. The invitation is not being given to you because you are in sin or have huge problems or are in a bad situation. It is simply that He wants you to leave the place where you are and come up to another place with Him.

Coming to Him means you leave what you are conscious of and become focused on and totally aware of only Him. This includes leaving, or laying down, a consciousness in your head of what you need to pray about. It means leaving a consciousness, or awareness, of whatever is demanding your attention in prayer. It means leaving a consciousness of all that the devil is doing around you. Why are you doing this? So that you can come up and get away from all those things and allow God Himself to fill all your consciousness.

A Dynamic Demonstration of His Power

There was a lady I traveled with in ministry for several years who God used to demonstrate His power in some of the most amazing ways. Miracles, signs and wonders were a regular occurrence. It wasn't just the miracles that were amazing, but also the supply of God's Spirit that manifested on the people in her services. Some people would just shake under the power of God.

Now, this woman didn't move in the gifts of the Spirit like we might think. Instead, she did normal things, like singing, and people were touched mightily by the power of God's Spirit. Without question, she was gifted by God with a beautiful voice. But unlike other singers, when this woman sang, things would happen to people that had never happened before. They experienced freedom, received healing and even had wonderful things take place in their children's lives.

One night, I distinctly remember a lady in the service whose teenage son had run away from home. When she returned to her house that night, he had come back because of the move of God in the service. During another series of meetings, there was a very timid minister who had a beautiful voice but was afraid to sing in front of others. Every time she did sing, she would cry. Consequently, she never wanted to do anything on the platform. But during those meetings, the power of God's Spirit that was manifesting changed her completely. This girl became freer and freer from the spirit of fear that had her bound. Initially, she got to the point where she would go up and sing on her own. Before long, all her stiffness was gone and she became animated when she sang. The change was amazing!

Needless to say, this woman minister I was traveling with was very fascinating to me because there was such a deep move of God wherever she went. I even remember people with sick or unruly animals that came to the meetings, and the flow of God's power brought healing to these people's pets. She was uniquely used by Him to bring the people in each service the specific things they needed. That is the anointing of God — it is God's Spirit supplying that which is needed.

Prepared in His Presence

Naturally, I was interested to see how she prepared for the services and learn about the different things she did in ministry. One day I asked her, "Do you pray about these things ahead of time? Do you have a deep desire to see certain things happen, or do you see these things happening in the Spirit and then pray about them and they come to pass in a church service?" She said, "No. I just *come to God.*"

So I learned this principle by experience. Before each meeting, we would simply come to God in prayer, which sometimes included conversation but most of the time meant we just came and sat in His presence. This was okay with everyone at the time, because we were in a hotel room preparing for a service. No one said anything or judged us. If you, as a believer, begin to come to God and just sit in His presence, you may receive persecution for it. Why? There will always be people who can label you as fanatical or out of touch with reality.

They will say things like, "What are you doing? What's the purpose in just sitting there doing nothing? Why are you wasting time? Are you lazy? Why do you do this? What happens when you do it?" Now stop for a moment and think: How would you answer questions like these if someone asked them?

The truth is, a lot of things that we do in our walk with God cannot be explained to others. We can only look into the Word of God as our example and examine Jesus' life to see how He lived. When we do, we will see that coming to God and sitting in His presence is a relevant way of accessing God's power that we must come to understand. In Christ, we receive things in our spirit that will never make sense from the world's point of view. This woman sitting still in the presence and power of God all day long is a perfect example.

CHAPTER 3

Be There!

Then the Lord said to Moses, *"Come up to Me* on the mountain and *be there*; and I will give you tablets of stone, and the law and commandments which I have written, that you may teach them."

Exodus 24:12 NKJV

At this point, the children of Israel needed the tablets of stone — they needed the laws and commandments of God. Although you and I don't need tablets of stone today, there are things that we do need. When God asks us to come up to Him, the things that we need will be given to us if we will just be there in His presence to receive them.

I think it's important to note that the words "be there" in Exodus 24:12 are in just about every translation of the Bible. At first, I thought these words were only in the Amplified translation, but when I looked, all the translations that I researched used the words *be there*.

Now, if you have *come* to a certain place, can you be anywhere else? If you have come up on a physical mountain, can you "be" in another place? I mean if you're there, then *you're there*, right? So what is God trying to say?

I believe what He is telling Moses (and us) is that when we come up into a "mountain," or a place of God's presence, we need to make ourselves very conscious of where we are. In other words, don't let your mind be in other places, focused on other things. Don't be distracted by what you need to pray about, what you need to confess, who has a problem, what is going on outside, or what may or may not happen in the world. Instead, just be there in spirit — be totally conscious of where you are. BE THERE!

When God created us, He made us a speaking spirit; so we are definitely going to speak to God. It's also important to realize that as the church, we're called to lift things up before the Lord in corporate prayer (Matthew 18:19). Actually, believers are the only people on the earth that have the ability to make a positive impact on the spirit realm in this hour. My purpose is not to negate anything that you may have been taught concerning corporate prayer.

What I am trying to do is simply introduce, establish and confirm another way in which we are to operate and move in God — simply by *coming to Him* and *being there* with Him. There is definitely a need for this kind of concentrated devotion to God in the times in which we live. Where else will you find your life but *in God?* As I said before, your life is hidden with Christ in God.

In Matthew 11:28, Jesus says,

> **Come to Me, all you who labor and are heavy laden, and I will give you rest.**
>
> (NKJV)

Just as God told Moses to come up to Him for the tablets of stone, Jesus is telling you and me to come to Him for what we need. If we are "heavy laden" and burdened by life and we come to Him, He will give us *rest.* We will not always be able to immediately explain or attach value to what God gives us or does in our lives while we are there in His presence. Nevertheless, our lives will always be tremendously blessed and better off because of it.

CHAPTER 4

Get in the Spirit

Looking back at Exodus 24:13-15 it says that

> ...Moses arose with his assistant Joshua, and Moses went up to the mountain of God. And he said to the elders, "Wait here for us until we come back to you. Indeed, Aaron and Hur are with you. If any man has a difficulty, let him go to them." Then Moses went up into the mountain, and a cloud covered the mountain.
>
> (NKJV)

I believe what God is saying to us in this passage is to *get into the Spirit*. For Moses, he went up, or climbed, a physical mountain. For us, we have access to God anytime, anywhere through the Holy Spirit and the blood of Jesus. Hallelujah!

Verse 16 goes on to say that once Moses went up into the mountain, "...the glory of the Lord rested on Mount Sinai, and the cloud covered it six days. And on the seventh day He called to Moses out of the midst of the cloud" (NKJV).

God knows all and sees all, therefore, He knows what is best for everyone at all times. He knew that the best thing for Moses and Joshua was to be in His presence for six days without talking before He gave them the law. Being in God's presence was what made them ready for their next step in Him.

Many times we accept Christ's invitation and we come to Him; but because we have so much to say, we quickly run out of breath because we are constantly talking and telling Him something. Yes, God's presence is a real place to pour out our heart to Him. However, what I'm describing to you here is something different. It is another facet of the way God operates that is very important; and that is, sometimes, all He wants is for you to just *come up to Him* and be there with Him.

Respond to the Light

"How long does God want me to be there?" you say. He wants you to *be there* until you quit responding to what is on the earth… He wants you to *be there* until you are not conscious of your soul… He wants you to *be there* until you are not responding out of your mind… He wants you to *be there* until you are not responding to anything the god of this world can contrive. God wants you to come to the place where you no longer respond to how you feel or what the devil or people are doing on the earth. Is this possible? Yes, it is by the power of His Spirit living inside you.

The fact is everything that you see going on around you in the natural is the result of what is happening in the spirit realm. It is either a reflection of the *dark* side, which is the spirit of the world, or the *light* side, which is the Spirit of God. So, since everything we see in the natural comes from the spirit, our lives consist of either responding to the spirit of the world or the Spirit of God.

Countless people in the world today are in such gross darkness; they are being controlled by the spirit of the world and don't even know it. You can look at their faces and see it in their eyes. With little or no effort at all, they respond to the dark side of the spirit all day long. Many people say that they don't know how to respond to the spirit. But the truth is, they are responding to the spirit all the time — it's just the negative or dark side they are responding to.

With so many negative things being said and done all around us every day, it's easy for us to get over into our emotions or mind and begin responding to the dark side of the spirit. Stop and think: What are the different negative things you tend to respond to? The good news is, you don't have to live like that. By God's grace, you can train your spirit to respond to the light side instead of the dark side. As a believer, you can *come* and connect yourself to God and His Holy Spirit and receive all that you need to respond and follow after Him.

So don't say that you don't know how to walk in the spirit because you do. You are more spirit than body, and the Lord has spent a lot of time training you to be sensitive to His Spirit. He is giving you this word right now so that you can know what is really going on. Oh, people may say that you're crazy or in a cult; but don't accept the label they put on you. You can know for sure that coming to God is where life comes from!

CHAPTER 5

Experiencing God's Glory

Again, think about Moses and Joshua on the mountain. The cloud covered Mt. Sinai for six days, and on the seventh day, the Lord called to Moses out of the midst of the cloud. For six days they were just *there*, and then on the seventh day God began to speak. Six days they sat in God's glory. What did they get during that time? I can't tell you. But whatever they received was the equipment they needed to do what God had called them to do.

Down in the camp, the glory of the Lord appeared to the Israelites like a devouring fire on top of the mountain. Now, while the glory of the Lord looked like a devouring fire to the Israelites, the Bible doesn't say what it looked like to Moses. At that time, Moses was not looking for fire or clouds — he was only looking for God.

Going back to the story I mentioned earlier about the minister I traveled with: Before each meeting, she and I "went up" and stayed in the presence of God for virtually the whole day. During those times, I could feel God's anointing on me. How did it feel? It felt like heaviness upon me physically, and all while we were preparing for the services, I would move in and out of His presence.

Of course, I had the notes of what I was going to preach with me, and from time to time I would look at them and think, *Oh, you better look them over and know these scriptures, or you won't be prepared to preach tonight.* The moment I did that, I would feel the anointing of God's presence lift off me.

At one point I remember waving my notes to God saying, "I don't know this…I don't have this message in my spirit, so how am I going to preach this?" Then, almost instantly, the Holy Spirit gently directed me back to quietly waiting in God's presence, and His heavy anointing returned. This is what it looked and felt like to me. What was the purpose in all this? I would soon find out.

Normally, I am a very strong willed person and don't like to get up in front of people unprepared. Miraculously, I was able to stay in the presence of the Lord. The Holy Spirit had so strongly presented Himself to me and affected my physical body, that I was convinced I needed to just *be there* in God's presence for His purposes. For what, you may ask? It was for my next step in Him. Could I have just gone ahead and studied my notes? Sure. But I, and others, would have missed out on experiencing God's glory.

Different Manifestations — Same Spirit

That night when we went to the service, there was a lady in the meeting who was terribly depressed. She later told us that a heavy depression often came upon her and caused her to become terribly afraid and depressed for months at a time. This manifestation of fear was so great that she couldn't leave her house. She said that occasionally it lifted and she was able to live a more normal life; but she always knew that it wasn't far away from her, and that eventually, it would return. This woman had fellowshipped with and examined this evil presence for so long that she could tell us everything about it. Sadly, she had become used to living with it.

Now keep in mind that I had been sitting in the presence of God all day, and He had done something wonderful in me. I was happy and still enjoying a good feeling of the heavy presence of God on me that evening. Again, this was what His presence felt like to me, and all that I had experienced while sitting with Him during the day had prepared me for the service that night.

That night in the meeting, I was actually ministering to the lady minister I was with. Suddenly, I sensed the glory of God upon me.

At that moment, I didn't say, "Oh, where are my notes? Give me the Scriptures I wrote down." No. I just chose to abide in His presence.

As I remained there, abiding in His presence, the lady who was battling the depression said something came down over her like white fire, and she couldn't see out of her eyes. She said it came down and it went back up and everything became clear. For the first time, she knew that the depression and fear were gone forever. This experience she had wasn't like the other ones in the past when the feeling would leave and she knew it would return. This time, it was completely gone!

So while my experience of God's glory manifested one way, this lady's experience of God's glory manifested another way altogether. As she responded to the Holy Spirit, the manifestation of God in her life brought forth freedom from the depression and fear. Somehow, God's glory was transformed in the Spirit onto her, giving her exactly what she needed. Praise God!

CHAPTER 6

The Evidence of Scripture

There are so many examples in Scripture of people who have had empowering experiences in God's presence. Actually, the Word of God is given to each of us so that we can look at it and know if we are on track or not. First Corinthians 10:11 says,

> **Now these things befell them by way of a figure [as as *example* and *warning* to us]; they were written to admonish and fit us for right action by good instruction, we in whose days the ages have reached their climax (their consummation and concluding period).**

One example given to us in Scripture is the life of Elijah. We see that there were a number of times in Elijah's life that he pulled away to spend time with God. For instance, there was the time when he stayed by the brook Cherith during a severe drought in the land of Israel. The Lord knew Elijah had to eat or he would die, so He brought ravens to feed him meat. Indeed, this was a big provisional miracle, but the most important thing Elijah did was to *stay with God*.

All during the time he spent there, God was doing a huge work in his life. I believe it was through these experiences in God's presence that the Lord prepared Elijah for the major outpourings of His Spirit that were ahead — like what took place on Mount Carmel (1 Kings

18:19-46). We know that on Mount Carmel, one of the most dramatic and dynamic miracles ever recorded in Scripture took place — fire came down from heaven and consumed both the sacrifice *and* the altar.

As Christians, we must understand that we don't have these kinds of results in God without spending time alone with Him. Search the Word and look at the great examples of people who often *came up* and spent time just *being there* with God. Interestingly, we know that when all the great events on Mount Carmel had ended and Elijah was threatened by Jezebel, he was overwhelmed with fear and ran for his life (1 Kings 19:1-4). I believe this proves that without a regular supernatural infusion of God, we will all fall flat on our face.

Jesus Was Transfigured in God's Presence

Another great example of the importance of coming *up* to God and just being there in His presence is found in the story of the transfiguration of Jesus. Look at Mark 9:2-4:

> **Six days after this, Jesus took with Him Peter and James and John and led them up on a high mountain apart *by themselves*. And He was transfigured before them and became resplendent with divine brightness. And His garments became glistening, intensely white, as no fuller (cloth dresser, launderer) on earth could bleach them. And Elijah appeared [there] to them, accompanied by Moses, and they were holding [a protracted] conversation with Jesus.**

Now, unlike Jesus, we are not necessarily looking for a physical mountain to climb in order to come up to God. But spiritually speaking, these words paint a powerful picture of what happens when we *come up* into God's presence.

First of all, when you climb a mountain, you make a decision to climb it with every step you take; as you climb, you go up in elevation. The same is not true when you go *down a road*. Your perspective is different when you look behind at all the things you've passed, and they become smaller and smaller the further you move away. As you look to the things in front of you, they seem to grow larger as you get closer to them.

But that is not how it is when you climb a mountain. With every step you take, you actually leave the place where you are and go up higher in elevation and perception. The panoramic view you get from above is impossible to have if you are just traveling down a flat road. When you increase in height, you have to make an effort to come up. But height always gives you an advantage.

I remember walking around Cape Martin near Menton France; with every step I took, I made a decision to go up. It is the same way in our relationship with God. With every step you take in His presence, you will always be conscious of your effort. Why? Because every step *up* in God will produce something new in you — a new advantage and a new understanding. Something will come out from God that you did not know, and it will be infused into you.

Realize that Jesus was not transfigured in a hole or in a valley; He went *up* on a mountain. It actually took Him and His three closest disciples time to climb it. Together, they all went up the mountain to get away by themselves and be with God. Through everything that took place, the glory of God was doing something miraculous that could not be put into words.

At a Loss for Words

Notice that here the Bible doesn't say much about any conversation on the mountain; it doesn't say anything about prayers going up or the disciples talking, yet, the manifestation of God's glory on Jesus still took place. Moses and Elijah appeared with Jesus, and His garments became dazzling white — much whiter than they could have ever been bleached. The Amplified translation says they were resplendent with divine brightness. Hallelujah!

Again, up until Mark 9:4 there wasn't any conversation. We really need to get this because normally when we look at and teach on the subject of communicating with God, we tend to "major" on the *sound* of prayer — the words we pray, how we pray, how we flow, etc. However, in our relationship with God there are also *silent times* with Him that we can't dismiss or pull away from. There are divine happenings and unexplained events that take place, that are relevant and rooted in our relationship with Him, but we will not be able to explain or put into words what God is doing during those times.

Look what happens in Mark 9:5-6.

> **And Peter took up the conversation, saying, Master, it is good and suitable and beautiful for us to be here. Let us make three booths (tents) — one for You and one for Moses and one for Elijah.** *For he did not [really] know what to say,* **for they were in a violent fright (aghast with dread).**

Have you ever been alone in God's presence and just not known what to say? Or maybe something was happening, but you really didn't know what it was? That is where Peter, James and John were.

In Mark 9:7-8 it goes on to say…

> **And a cloud threw a shadow upon them, and a voice came out of the cloud, saying, This is My Son, the [most dearworthy] Beloved One.** *Be constantly listening to* **and** *obeying Him!* **And looking around, they suddenly no longer saw anyone with them except Jesus only.**

Something miraculous happened; a cloud of God's presence descended, the voice of God spoke, and Elijah and Moses went away, leaving Jesus there alone with them. "And as they were coming back down the mountain, He admonished and expressly ordered them to tell no one what they had seen until the Son of Man should rise from among the dead. So they carefully and faithfully kept the matter to themselves…" (Mark 9:9-10).

Two Worlds Collide

Shortly thereafter, Jesus, Peter, James and John find the other nine disciples and come upon them in the midst of a major dispute. Amazingly, the glory of what took place on the mountain was still very apparent on Jesus and evident to all. Mark 9:15 says, "And immediately all the crowd, when they saw Jesus [returning from the holy mount,

His face and person yet glistening], they were greatly amazed and ran up to Him [and] greeted Him."

Jesus then asks His disciples and the others close by what they were questioning and discussing with the Scribes. Mark 9:17-18 fills us in on what was going on:

> And one of the throng replied to Him, Teacher, I brought my son to You, for he has a dumb spirit. And wherever it lays hold of him [so as to make him its own], it dashes him down and convulses him, and he foams [at the mouth] and grinds his teeth, and he [falls into a motionless stupor and] is wasting away. And I asked Your disciples to drive it out, and they were not able [to do it].

So after Jesus and His three closest disciples experienced a manifestation of God's glory on the mountain, a manifestation of another kind was about to take place down below. A demonic spirit that had taken possession of a young man much earlier in his life, was unable to be cast out by the other nine disciples. In great distress and despair, the boy's father sought Jesus to bring deliverance. After Jesus reprimanded His followers for their lack of faith, He called for the boy to be brought to Him.

> So they brought [the boy] to Him, and when the spirit saw Him, at once it completely convulsed the boy, and he fell to the ground and kept rolling about, foaming [at the mouth].
>
> And [Jesus] asked his father, How long has he had this? And he answered, From the time he was a little boy. And it has often thrown him both into fire and into water, intending to kill him. But if You can do anything, do have pity on us and help us.
>
> And Jesus said, [You say to Me], If You can do anything? [Why,] all things can be (are possible) to him who believes!
>
> **Mark 9:20-23**

Then when Jesus saw that a crowd of people was gathering, "… He rebuked the unclean spirit, saying to it, You dumb and deaf spirit, I charge you to come out of him and never go into him again" (Mark 9:25). And the spirit came out of the boy with a shriek.

At this point, the disciples were dumbfounded over the situation and decided to pull Jesus aside and ask Him why they couldn't drive out the evil spirit. I think this shows us that as disciples of Christ, we all need to pull Him aside at times and ask Him questions so that we can understand the things that are going on. Amen!

Listen to how Jesus answered them. He said, "...This kind cannot be driven out by anything but prayer and fasting" (Mark 9:29). Now not all translations include the word fasting. But fasting, like anything else in our walk with God, is something we do when we feel led by the Spirit to do it. For now, we are not going to look any deeper into the subject of fasting. However, what I do want to take a closer look at is how Jesus actually dealt with this situation.

First of all, it is important to know that this deaf and dumb spirit is also referred to in Matthew 17:15 as *epilepsy* (or *seizures* in some translations). The interesting thing is that epilepsy, according to the word's original meaning, is also known as a condition known as *moonstruck*. This spirit of epilepsy is said to increase when the moon becomes full and decrease as it wanes.

Hopefully, this helps you see even more how things in the spirit *explode* on things in the natural. The spirit realm is not way "out there" somewhere; it is here all around us, and it is influenced by things in the natural realm and vice versa. Think about it: If the moon has influence on the realm of the spirit, what influence do *you* have on the spirit realm? What effect do you, the one who God has created as a speaking spirit and has given all power and authority to, have on the spirit realm (Luke 10:19)?

Again, Jesus tells His disciples that this kind of spirit is not driven out any other way but by prayer. Yet, we don't see that Jesus actually prayed for this epileptic boy. In fact, Jesus never prayed for anyone to be healed. On the contrary, He *commanded* them to be healed. So what does Jesus mean when He says this kind only comes out through prayer? When would He have been prepared by prayer to handle this specific incident? I believe He was prepared in God's presence during His time up on the mountain.

The Power of the Glory

Did you know that anything that comes into contact with the glory of God just collapses under the power of the Glory? The glory of God repels demons; no demon can stay in the presence of the Glory. Jesus said this kind doesn't come out except by prayer, and we see that He was in the presence of God at the beginning of this chapter, being glorified up on the mountain.

Look at what Jesus says about being glorified in John 17:1-2

> **...Father, the hour has come. Glorify and exalt and honor and magnify Your Son, so that Your Son may glorify and extol and honor and magnify You. [Just as] You have granted Him power and authority over all flesh (all humankind), [now glorify Him] so that He may give eternal life to all whom You have given Him.**

I believe what this is saying is that we cannot and will not glorify God unless *He first glorifies us*. We have to get into the place where He does the glorifying. I only know of one situation in the Bible where the glory of God ran a man down, and that is in the story of Saul (Acts 9:1-9). God appeared to him on the road to Damascus, he became a believer, his name was changed to Paul, and he became one of the greatest apostles that ever lived. Virtually every other time God performed mighty acts on the earth it was in connection with His people pulling away to spend time in His presence.

Far too often the emphasis has been placed on what we need to *do* in order to see God's glory manifested. Well, the most important thing we need to do is pull away and *come up* into God's presence and just be there so that He can prepare us for opportunities to manifest His glory. How will His Glory manifest? It will manifest in such a way that a continual supply of God *flowing through you and me* will supply people's needs and also their desires.

Now, you may feel like Peter did up on the mountain of transfiguration, wanting to capture God's glory and just stay there with Him, but you can't. Like Jesus told Peter and the others, He says to us today: "Come on guys...we have work to do. We have to come down from here and go to the others so that they too may see the glory of God manifested."

59

Take the Challenge!

Don't ever feel condemned about waiting on God. When we wait on Him, great things take place and He releases His power and strength into our lives. Isaiah 40:29-31 says,

> **He gives power to the weak, and to those who have no might He increases strength.**
> **Even the youths shall faint and be weary, and the young men shall utterly fall,**
> **But those who *wait* on the Lord shall renew their strength; they shall mount up with wings like eagles, they shall run and not be weary, they shall walk and not faint. (NKJV)**

This word *wait* here means "to braid," which gives us a picture of being intertwined with God just like hair is braided and woven together. The Amplified version of verse 31 says that those who *wait* on the Lord "…shall change and renew their strength and power; they shall lift their wings and mount up [close to God] as eagles [mount up close to the sun]; they shall run and not be weary, they shall walk and not faint or become tired." Hallelujah!

There are many more examples of waiting in the presence of God in the Word. I encourage you to study them out for yourself. Learn how time spent in the presence of the Lord is vital to finishing your course. In His presence is fullness of joy, and the joy of the Lord is your strength! While you are there before Him, His glory will equip you to run your race and do what you could never do in your own strength. I challenge you to set aside time regularly to just come and be with God and allow Him to change and empower you for His purposes!

HOW TO CAST YOUR CARES

Introduction

Have you ever noticed that you rarely see teaching tapes or books entitled *Faith Secrets* or *Healing Secrets*, yet you can find all sorts of teaching materials that talk about "*prayer* secrets"? There is actually good reason for this, for there has always been a great deal of ignorance among Christians about the subject of prayer.

However, we cripple our spiritual walk if we are satisfied to remain in ignorance. It should be our goal to *discover* those prayer secrets, which were never meant to remain hidden, but to be shouted from the housetops! They are keys in God that, if followed, can make us successful in every area of life.

One of these keys is to pray Spirit-led prayers. In order to do this, a believer has to go into the realms of the Spirit with faith and with the word of God. This is one of the strongest expectations God has of His people: that they know how to communicate with Him and work with His Spirit in prayer.

> Pray at all times (on every occasion, in every season) in the Spirit, with all [manner of] prayer and entreaty. To that end keep alert and watch with strong purpose and perseverance, interceding on behalf of all the saints (God's consecrated people).
>
> Ephesians 6:18

In every season of your life, you are called to *pray in the Spirit*. This means you are to be led by the Holy Spirit in all manner of prayer and entreaty. *To that end*, Paul says that you are to keep alert and watch. To what end? To the end of prayer — to the end of every season and every occasion during which you are praying — you must keep alert and watch, developing the attributes of strong purpose and a persevering spirit.

Notice the last phrase in this verse: "…interceding on behalf of all the saints." The prayer of intercession is just one kind of prayer that you are to pray, primarily for those who are lost. It involves standing in the gap for someone. Since there *is* no gap between believers and God, those in the Church don't need you to stand in the gap for them.

Have you ever heard someone say, "I'm an intercessor"? There is a problem with that statement, because a person is a *pray-er*, not an intercessor. Intercession is just *one* manner or kind of prayer. There are other kinds of prayer found in the Bible as well, such as the prayer of supplication, the prayer of agreement, the prayer of faith, and the prayer of consecration. It is possible in prayer that is led by the Holy Spirit to encompass all of these kinds of prayer; otherwise, God would not have put this verse in the Bible.

In this book, I endeavor to bring to light a particular kind of prayer that affects your personal fellowship with God and thus affects your call and your outward place of ministry. I'm talking about the prayer of *casting your cares upon the Lord*. Although this is not the kind of prayer you will regularly pray in a prayer group, it is nevertheless extremely vital to your life of faith. As we explore what it means to pour out your heart before God, we will also look at another critical kind of prayer that is tied closely to the prayer *of casting your cares*.

The kinds of personal prayer we will talk about are secrets that God always intended for you to discover and to walk in every day of your life. As you read this book, that is exactly what you will learn how to do.

Lucy McKee

CHAPTER I

Personal Fellowship

Prayer is directed toward God in two basic arenas: in *personal fellowship* and in *corporate prayer*. Even though these two types of prayer operate hand-in-hand with each other, there are distinct differences between them. As in all of life, there is an order that works best. "First things first" is a principle that applies to prayer.

Corporate prayer is where we do business with God in a setting with other believers. This is not a time to practice casting our cares on God or to seek Him about our own personal issues. However, these latter two types of prayer *are* important, and we will never be effective in the corporate setting until we develop our own personal prayer life before God.

That is why it is so vital that we learn how to seek God for our own answers before we come to the corporate prayer group. There is a correlation between trusting God with our personal concerns and His ability to flow through us in prayer for the "large" prayer projects in which God would like to use us in these last days. In fact, it is impossible for us to pray effectively for nations and kings if we don't know how to get our own personal needs met or how to cast our cares on the Lord.

The Weight of Your Cares
Is Not Yours to Carry

We often find that it is easier to do business with God in prayer for other people than it is to obtain answers for ourselves. We have no problem going before God's throne to say, "Lord, we pray for Brother So-and-so. We lift up his need to You, confidently expecting You to move on his behalf." Meanwhile, the difficult circumstances we face in our own lives can often seem insurmountable when it's time for us to take them before the Father's throne in prayer.

Certainly, it is very important for us to pray for others. However, we must also be able to leave our own cares and concerns with God; otherwise, we cannot remain effective in our prayers that extend outward. That is why the Word of God teaches us about the prayer of *casting our cares on the Lord.*

> **Casting the whole of your care [all your anxieties, all your worries, all your concerns, once and for all] on Him, for He cares for you affectionately and cares about you watchfully.**
>
> **1 Peter 5:7**

Notice that this kind of prayer involves casting *all* of your worries and anxieties on the Lord — every single thing in your life that you fret about. You must learn how to throw these cares over on God once and for all, so that the weight of these burdens is *no longer yours* to carry, but *His* alone.

This is the principle in which we operate in the natural when we have a burden, such as a heavy package or suitcase, that we are trying to carry or move. For instance, in my travels over the years, I have had to take suitcases that I couldn't even lift off the floor. If it had solely been up to me to transport those suitcases, I would have been forced to leave them where they sat! But I always had a plan: I'd look for someone else who was bigger and stronger than I to carry my heavy suitcases where they needed to go.

It is easy in this kind of natural situation to cast the burden off on someone else because you can actually see that person. You can see how physically capable he is to carry that load. But here is what you have to realize: God is right there with you. He is telling you, "…I will never leave you nor forsake you" (Hebrews 13:5 *NKJV*). And He wants you to give Him *all* your cares and concerns and stop trying to carry them by yourself.

Why is it so hard for us to remember to cast our cares on the Lord? It's so easy to hand over a heavy burden in the natural realm to someone who is stronger than we are because seeing is believing. It is very difficult for our natural minds to roll something we *can* see on Someone we *can't* see.

Yet, our success in prayer depends on our learning to do exactly that. Our effectiveness in praying for nations, for the Church, or for our communities is directly dependent on how well we are able to release our personal cares and concerns into the hands of God. When we can readily see Him taking care of the personal issues we are facing in life, it will be easier for us to believe Him for the alignment of nations, world revival, the harvest of souls, and all of His end-time plans and purposes for humanity.

It is crucial that we see this correlation between our responsibility to trust God to provide our personal answers and our ability to believe Him to be able to handle the problems of the world. We simply cannot be effective in praying for others if we can't trust Him with our own personal concerns.

We'll never get anywhere in prayer with an attitude that says, "You take those issues, God, and I will deal with this one. I can handle it on my own." All too often, that is exactly how we try to manage our lives in God, and it is the reason we too often fail.

Fellowship vs. Relationship

This is the truth we have to grasp in our walk with God: We are not trying to endear Him to us; we just need the revelation that He is *already* endeared to us. The Word tells us that He is.

God loves you more than any other person could ever love you. He loved you enough to send His Son to be born on this earth and to live His entire life as a Man so He could bear your sins and die in your place. So if God is already endeared to you, what is the real issue? It is that *you must endear yourself to your Heavenly Father.* And you do this the same way you would endear yourself to any other person: through *communication.*

Every relationship in every realm of life — in your family, your circle of friends, your business, your church — is built and maintained on communication. If you don't really like someone, do you care if you ever talk to that person? No, you don't. But when you want to become better acquainted with someone you love, you spend time with that person and begin to share your thoughts and your hearts with one another. In the same way, your fellowship with God will mature and develop as you learn how to communicate with Him more and more.

Many Christians assume that they automatically have power with God to ask Him for the souls of men. But this is actually not the case, if, in their own hearts, these same Christians cannot trust God with all their fears, worries, anxieties, and cares. They must *know* that He is faithful to carry their concerns and is not only able but willing to do something about those concerns. However, this kind of trust is developed only through true fellowship with God.

There is a huge difference between relationship and fellowship. We all came in relationship with God as our Father the moment we were born again. So the question is not about our relationship with Him. The Father provided the way to have that relationship through the redemptive work of His Son Jesus on the cross.

However, Jesus cannot provide your fellowship with the Father, nor can He determine how intimate and passionate that fellowship will be on a daily basis. Only *you* can do that. Only you can provide the correct answer to the question, *Who is your first love?*

Proverbs 3:5 (*NKJV*) instructs you to "trust in the Lord with all your heart, and lean not on your own understanding." When you begin to exercise your faith by casting all your cares on the Lord, you are learning what it means to obey that scripture. However, you must remember that your faith works by love (Galatians 5:6). It is only as you make the Father your first Love, and begin putting that kind of love to work in prayer that you come to a place in Him where *nothing* in this life can stop you. This is the reason it is so very important for you to learn how to communicate with God.

To endear yourself to your Heavenly Father's heart, fellowship with Him has to be personal *first*. And you have to keep pursuing intimacy with the Father until your time spent with Him becomes the most desirable place you could ever be. It has to be more desirable than:

- Being with your children and family.
- Cleaning your house.
- Having the satisfaction of seeing your supper cooked and everything in place by two o'clock in the afternoon.
- Enjoying social and physical activities
- Seeing your business become a success.
- Developing and administrating your ministry.

There is a place in your walk with God where *everything you do every moment of the day is done so you can be with Him*. That is the place you want to reach, for only then will you be able to declare with a full and honest heart, "...It is no longer I who live, but Christ lives in me; and the life which I now live in the flesh I live by faith in the Son of God..." (Galatians 2:20).

CHAPTER 2

Get to the Root

If you truly pray in faith, you will always receive an answer from God. This is true regardless of the situation you face or the realm of life you are praying about — family, job, marriage, finances, church, or physical and mental health. It is entirely possible to grow to a place in your prayer life where you *always* receive answers to your prayers.

I know this to be true from personal experience. I also know that the answer we receive from the Lord may not always be the one we want to hear.

When it comes to casting our cares on the Lord, it can be troubling to realize that the issues in our lives we are so concerned about will not suddenly be worked out in a moment of time. This is when a concern often becomes a *care*. We want to see the symptoms changed, but God is more interested in our dealing with the *root cause* behind the symptoms.

For example, some people never seem to have enough money to pay their bills. That state of chronic lack is only a symptom of a deeper root problem, such as poor financial management, laziness, or the pursuit of wrong things. As long as the root cause isn't dealt with, the symptoms will persist and these people will sink deeper and deeper into debt. The burden of debt, then, becomes a care that continually weighs them down and keeps them from going forward in their walk with God.

Many times wrong thinking is at the root of our cares, worries, and fears. When this is the case, God isn't interested in merely correcting the situation or the symptom. He doesn't just pull us out of the big mess we see in front of our natural eyes. God wants to correct the wrong thinking that got us into that mess in the first place! He knows that this is how He can best serve us.

He Gives You What You Need

It is true that the Lord will often use other people's voices to amplify a truth you need to learn or a problem you need to deal with in your life. However, what He really desires is for you to learn how to address Him directly, and how to recognize His voice when He addresses *you*. Every day He will tell you what you need to know about each particular concern on your heart.

Many times we get impatient and ask, "Why won't You completely remove this care from my life, God?" We are consumed with our own efforts to get rid of the problem we face, but the answer to our need is often a process. First, God has to work out our wrong thinking. Meanwhile, He calls us to rest in the confidence that He is going to give us each day what we need.

What is it that you need today?

Some days you will need the Lord to confront you about the areas in your life you haven't yet surrendered to Him.

Other days you will need to be lifted up and encouraged.

There will be still other days when you will need God to comfort you.

And on many days, you will need God to come in and change the way you're thinking. On any given day, He will give you what you need.

Building the Platform For Victory

Over the course of our lives, we learn to respond in certain ways when faced with certain situations. Psychologists called these specific patterns of behavior "learned responses." Like grooves in a screw, these patterns form "grooves" in our souls, and our thoughts and emotions tend to fall into these predetermined ruts whenever we're confronted with a particular challenge or difficult circumstance.

The Holy Spirit dwells within you to renew your mind and transform you to line up with His ways. He wants *you* to see the connection between a lack of time management and never having enough money to pay your bills — between the carnal pattern and the undesirable result. God goes for the root of the problem and begins to change the way you think. He knows that your renewed mind will eventually change your behavior.

The devil will try to build traps in your life, using your wrong thinking, worries, and fears as building material. Perhaps you have been trying to get free of these mental strongholds for years, yet again and again, you seem to keep bumping back into them. You cry out to God to take those wrong thoughts away from you, but there never seems to be any change. These things frustrate and embarrass you, making you feel like you are constantly stumbling in your spiritual race and scraping your shins. Finally, you start feeling like you will never be free.

However, your Heavenly Father can take the cruelest traps of the enemy and turn them into the most glorious victories of your life. God begins by looking at the big picture rather than at the little problems you are currently facing. Meanwhile, He changes your thinking, building a platform in your renewed mind from which to launch you out of the very problem that the devil is trying to erect as a trap to ensnare you. That divine platform will have more width, length, and depth to it than any trap the enemy could ever use against you, enabling you to minister to others in ways you were never able to before.

Do you remember Haaman in the book of Esther? Haaman built a set of gallows from which to hang Esther's uncle Mordecai. But who was later hung on those same gallows? Haaman himself! He was actually hung on the very death trap he had built for someone else.

In the same way, all the obstacles that keep tripping you up will be the very things God uses to build you into the yielded vessel He needs to minister to others. The devil may try to use your weaknesses to build gallows upon which to hang you, but those weaknesses will be the very areas of your life from which you will be able to hang *him*. The devil has always been good at building the means for his own demise.

The cross was the biggest "gallows" that the devil ever built, and when we walk in obedience to the Lord, we hang Satan on those gallows every single day that we live! That victory keeps working for us over and over again. Yet, look at how long it took for God to work out His plan of redemption — all the way from the fall of man in Genesis 3 to the day Jesus breathed His Spirit on His disciples in John 20!

"Oh, God," you might plead, "don't let it be that long before You answer my needs and remove all my cares!"

It *won't* be that long, for we don't have that much time left. Besides, God has much weightier concerns for you to pray about than those personal cares that seem so difficult and terrible to you right now. He is interested in helping you overcome every problem that has hindered you in the past so you can focus your energies on praying out His plans and purposes for the days ahead!

CHAPTER 3

One Master

No one can serve two masters; for either he will hate the one and love the other, or he will stand by and be devoted to the one and despise and be against the other...

Matthew 6:24

Jesus said that you cannot serve two masters. That means you are either going to serve your cares, your frets, your worries, and your fears — or you are going to serve the living God. It has to be one or the other, because you can't serve both.

The Choice
Between Faith and Fear

We must also make the choice between *faith* and *fear* on a daily basis. The Scriptures tell us that faith works by love, that perfect love casts out fear, and that God *is* love (Galatians 5:6; 1 John 4:16,18). As we fellowship with God, we learn to trust in His love, and to a greater and greater degree, how to cast our cares upon Him. Fear simply cannot live in that kind of environment!

This was the essence of Jesus' message in Matthew 6:

> Therefore I tell you, stop being perpetually uneasy (anxious and worried) about your life, what you shall eat or what you shall drink; or about your body, what you shall put on. Is not life greater [in quality] than food, and the body [far above and more excellent] than clothing?
>
> Look at the birds of the air; they neither sow nor reap nor gather into barns, and yet your heavenly Father keeps feeding them. Are you not worth much more than they?
>
> Matthew 6:25-27

Why are we much more valuable than the birds? Because Jesus died for us. We are His pearl of great price, purchased by His own precious blood.

This verse also tells us that we are important because we do sow, we do reap, and we do gather into barns.

> And why should you be anxious about clothes? Consider the lilies of the field and learn thoroughly how they grow; they neither toil nor spin. Yet I tell you, even Solomon in all his magnificence (excellence, dignity, and grace) was not arrayed like one of these.
>
> Matthew 6:28,29

We put so much anxious energy into pursuing natural riches in this life — yet look at what God says about the lilies of the field. They are better clothed than King Solomon was in all of his glory!

> But if God so clothes the grass of the field, which today is alive and green and tomorrow is tossed into the furnace, will He not much more surely clothe you, O you of little faith?
>
> Therefore do not worry and be anxious, saying, What are we going to have to eat? or, What are we going to have to drink? or, What are we going to have to wear?
>
> Matthew 6:30,31

The bottom line that Jesus is trying to get across to us in these verses is simple: "Little faith" reasons and worries instead of trusting the Lord.

Trusting God
For Spiritual Food and Clothing

People ask the kinds of anxious questions found in verse 31 not only in their natural lives, but also in their spiritual lives. They'll ask, "What is our meal going to be in church today? Who is going to feed us?" Then they'll often say something like, "Oh, is *he* preaching tonight? I don't receive much from him. I was hoping for the other preacher."

We also get anxious about how we are spiritually clothed. If God speaks to us to do something out of our comfort zone, we often think, "*Oh, what am I going to wear to do that? How am I going to wear that anointing?*"

The Word says we groan in our spirit to be further clothed (1 Corinthians 5:4 *NKJV*). But does that phrase "further clothed" mean wearing expensive shoes and a new dress? No. It means *to be clothed with the anointing of the Holy Spirit.*

It is true that you have to be clothed with the Holy Spirit's anointing in order to minister to people. But you don't get "further clothed" by entertaining anxious thoughts about your natural inadequacies! Walking in close fellowship with the Father is the only way you will stay fully dressed in the Spirit for whatever situation arises.

Take No Thought of Worry

As we continue in this passage, we find Jesus' answer to living a life free from worry and anxiety:

> **For the Gentiles (heathen) wish for and crave and diligently seek all these things, and your heavenly Father knows well that you need them all.**
>
> **But seek (aim at and strive after) first of all His kingdom and His righteousness (His way of doing and being right), and then all these things taken together will be given you besides. So do not worry or be anxious about tomorrow, for tomorrow will have worries and anxieties of its own. Sufficient for each day is its own trouble.**
>
> **Matthew 6:32-34**

The word "kingdom" carries the connotation of a nation with many colonies, such as England. But God's Kingdom is made up of righteousness, peace, and joy in the Holy Ghost (Romans 14:17). This Kingdom operates according to *God's* ways of doing and being right.

In this passage about God's Kingdom, we are told five times to stop being anxious or worried. The *King James Version* says it this way in verse 34: "Take therefore no thought for the morrow...." I like that. We are instructed by the Lord not to *take* worry thoughts, depression thoughts, or sickness thoughts and make them our own, allowing them to take up residence in our minds.

The Word tells us that worry is a sin. It is motivated out of fear, not faith, and *everything* that is done outside of faith is a sin.

You might say, "But you don't know what I am going through! If I don't worry about this situation, who will?" Regardless of what you're going through, the Word firmly instructs you to "take no thought" about your life.

How do we "take" thoughts? By *saying* them. If we talk all the time about what we see or feel instead of what the Word of God says about a particular situation, our words will lead us down the path of worry. It is as we speak our concerns and worries out of our mouths that the actual "*taking*" process occurs.

To stop this process of taking thoughts of worry, we are going to have to operate the same principle in the positive — speaking other things besides what we are worried about. We are called to *take* the thoughts of God — found in His Word — and to *speak* them.

That is how you cast down the imaginations that arise in your mind day and night. You don't do it by replacing thoughts with thoughts. The way you take a worry thought is by speaking it, and the way you are going to take *God's* thoughts is by speaking His Word out of your mouth.

Cleaning Out
Your Spiritual Closet

Is it best to just try to avoid thoughts of worry and anxiety?

- Should we get so busy with our daily schedules that we don't have time to look at the worrisome circumstances in our lives?

- Should we take up a hobby or go on vacation to escape what we don't want to think about?
- Should we sit down in front of the TV with the remote control and lose ourselves in the images of Hollywood?

No! The Bible is not telling us to be irresponsible and to ignore what is going on in front of us. "Taking no thought" doesn't mean we are to cover over all our problems with denial or self-deceived optimism.

Have you ever crammed something in a closet to hide it and then had to slam the door to get it to stay closed? In that kind of situation, the solution is *not* to wedge a chair under the door handle to keep the closet closed. All that overstuffed closet really needs is a good cleaning out. There are far too many things crowded in there — such as brooms, a vacuum cleaner, old detergent, maybe even trash.

What is the best way to clean out that kind of messy closet? You need to pull everything out and sort through it all to see what is worth keeping, what needs to be given to someone else, and what needs to be thrown away.

Our minds can be like that "bursting at the seams" closet — filled with good and bad thoughts all mixed together. And far too often, we do our best to ignore our negative thoughts instead of doing something about them.

However, God commands you to *capture* your thoughts of worry and fear. Bring them out and examine them. Get all of that mess cleaned out of your mind so you can start doing what God needs you to do!

Throw away the thoughts that need to be thrown away. Delegate to others the issues that someone else can take care of so you don't have to think about them anymore. If you don't, you will end up thinking about those issues again, and just like a big vacuum, you will suck those cares right back on you.

God is big enough and capable enough to do something great with our lives. But we will only begin to realize the greatness of His good plan for us as we learn how to clean out our spiritual closet and cast *all* of our cares upon Him, once and for all.

CHAPTER 4

Clothed In Humility

God shows us in His Word the attitude of heart that causes Him to move on our behalf.

> ...CLOTHE (APRON) YOURSELVES, ALL OF YOU, WITH HUMILITY [as the garb of a servant, so that its covering cannot possibly be stripped from you, with freedom from pride and arrogance] toward one another. For God sets Himself against the proud (the insolent, the overbearing, the disdainful, the presumptuous, the boastful) — [and He opposes, frustrates, and defeats them], but gives grace (favor, blessing) to the humble.
>
> 1 Peter 5:5

God honors the heart that is clothed with humility. We are to submit to one another. More importantly, we are to submit to God and His Word. This, then, frees us from pride and arrogance and puts us in a position to receive God's grace and favor.

What Does It Mean
To Humble Yourself?

Pride is a major hindrance to our success as sons of God in the earth. Therefore, the first thing we must do is to *humble ourselves*.

> **Therefore humble yourselves [demote, lower yourselves in your own estimation] under the mighty hand of God, that in due time He may exalt you, casting the whole of your care [all your anxieties, all your worries, all your concerns, once and for all] on Him, for He cares for you affectionately and cares about you watchfully.**

> **1 Peter 5:6,7**

Humbling yourself involves turning to God for your answer instead of trying to come up with the answer on your own. It is saying, "God, I'm fresh out of good ideas. I cannot solve this myself."

People often have a distorted view of what it means to humble one's self. They think it means that they are supposed to belittle themselves or grovel before God's throne and beg Him to hear them. Some also hold to the belief that God wants to "take them down a notch."

But here is what you have to remember: God does not humble you. No one else can humble you. You have to humble *yourself*.

You may think that this verb "humble" means to let yourself get run over by other people. But that isn't what that word means at all. I'm not talking about your getting humbled by someone else. When that happens, it usually means you're being *humiliated* rather than truly humbled.

I am also not talking about someone else coming to you and counseling you. Yes, God expects your spiritual leaders to come to you if they see something in your life that is leading you to destruction. But it isn't their job to humble you. You must humble *yourself*.

The First Step
in Humbling Yourself

How do you do that? What *is* humbling yourself? First Peter 5:8 (*NKJV*) tells you: "Therefore humble yourselves under the mighty hand of God...CASTING ALL YOUR CARE UPON HIM...."

82

To admit, "I don't know what to do, Lord," is the starting point of humility. It is the proud person who will not call out to God for help — and pride is the very sin that got the devil kicked out of Heaven. Pride is an extremely serious offense in the eyes of God.

Pride says, "This is what I'm going to do to handle this problem" or "I know how to deal with this difficult person — I'll say this!"

If that is how you typically deal with challenges in your life, you are leaning on your own understanding. When you humble yourself, you decide, *I will go to God first. I will cast the care of this situation on Him and find out what He wants me to do. I won't wait until after I have run out of everything I can do on my own before I put my trust in the Lord to perfect that which concerns me.*

So humble yourself before the Lord. Cast all your cares on Him once and for all, and refuse to carry them any longer all by yourself. This is the ultimate act of humility, for in casting your cares on God, you are stating, "Without Him, I can do nothing. But with Him, I can do all things!"

CHAPTER 5

Empty the Dump Truck!

You probably know what it's like to have people unload all their problems on you. It's as if they are driving a dump truck in reverse, and suddenly they empty their entire truckload of emotional garbage on top of you!

If you've ever been in that situation, you know that something feels very wrong about it. Here's why you feel that way: God is continually inviting every believer to back up his or her "dump truck of cares" to His throne and unload it all on *Him*.

How Do We Unload Our Cares On God?

Is dumping our load of cares on God just a matter of saying, "Lord, I praise and magnify You"? No. Although praise is a powerful part of our prayer life, it is not in itself effective in casting the cares from our minds and our hearts. We can't truly praise until we release those weights and cares unto the Lord.

So are we unloading our cares on the Lord when we say, "Thank You, Jesus, oh, thank You, Jesus"? No, we are expressing our gratitude to Jesus for what He has done for us. But that is *not* casting our cares on the Lord.

What if we cry really hard about the problems we're facing? That may release some emotional pressure, but it accomplishes little to nothing in releasing our cares to the Lord.

Now, there *is* a place in God where the Holy Spirit will lead you to weep and travail in prayer. These are times when words won't come as you pray and all you can do is weep. When that occurs, you should yield to that leading and allow the Holy Spirit to develop this type of travailing prayer in you. But that isn't what I'm talking about here. I am referring to a whiny form of crying that has no substance to it. That is definitely *not* what it means to cast your cares on the Lord.

The same people who will unload their problems on you in intricate detail are usually very abstract when they come to God about those same problems. But if a person is ever going to get rid of his cares, he will have to learn how to very deliberately place those cares into the hands of the Almighty God. After all, God is the only One who can do something about them!

So, how *do* we cast our cares on the Lord? We do the same thing we do when we cast our cares on our friends! *We tell God what our specific cares are.* This is so simple that we miss it.

Be Yourself with God

Too often when people pray, they seldom act like themselves. When they talk to God about a problem in their lives, they go into a vague, formal mode, praying something like this: "Oh, Lord God, I casteth on Thee these cares and ask that Thou wouldst move on my behalf."

You are created in the image of God, so consider how *you'd* feel if someone talked like that to you. Well, God responds the same way. He's saying, "Just be yourself with Me. Talk to Me the way you talk to your friends. And which one of your cares are you even talking about? How can I help you if you are not specific in your request?"

You might say, "*I* don't know which care I'm talking about, God, but *You* know."

The truth is, you do know which care you're talking about, because you probably just got off the phone after telling your friend all about it!

86

So why can't you tell *God* all about it? He is the only One big enough to handle the problem.

You have probably heard someone pray like this: "Oh, God, oh, God, have You noticed my husband? Lord, have You noticed? Oh, God, *do* something about my husband, O Lord!" Can you imagine talking to your friends like that? Would you say to your friend, "Oh, Betty, oh, Betty, oh, Betty"? If you did, she would think that you were strange!

Yet we use that kind of religious language all the time with our Heavenly Father. *The point I'm trying to make is that we need to learn to be as specific and real with God as we are with our spouse or our closest friends.*

Cut through all the religious language, and just talk to the Lord from your heart, sharing with Him every detail of what is going on in your life. Make this a daily practice so cares and worries don't start stacking up on your mental desk.

When you cast your cares on other people, they tell you what they think about it. You could go from person to person to person and get a different opinion every time. But if you will go to God, He will give you *His* opinion, and His will be the *right* opinion. In fact, He is going to give you the wisdom of the ages — a Word in due season just for you.

What Matters to You Matters to God

There is a big downside to talking about your cares with other people: The problems or concerns that are huge to you often seem small to them. But if those cares are important enough to occupy your soul twenty four hours a day, they are *big* concerns. If they weren't so important to you, you wouldn't be worrying so much about them!

The situations and problems you're facing matter to you; therefore, they matter to God — because *you* matter to Him. He cares about *everything* that concerns you. That is what the Word says.

When you hold on to cares and concerns, they will bother you in your soul, keeping you so occupied that you never step out to fulfill the call of God on your life. You can't effectively pursue your divine call as long as those cares are weighing you down.

So back up the dump truck to God's throne, and unload all your cares on Him. Talk to Him as you would your best friend, telling Him about every care in intricate detail; then listen in your heart for what He has to say to you. In His response will be the divine wisdom you need to be set free from worry and positioned for victory in every situation.

CHAPTER 6

Build Up Your Confidence
In God

Let me give you a key that will help you cast all your cares on the Lord. This is something I've learned over the years in my own walk with God.

Often before you can pull your cares out of your heart and cast them onto God, you will have to meditate on some scriptures that guarantee His love and His concern for you. *Build up your faith in the truth that He is your answer.*

We can understand this principle better if we relate it once again to the natural realm. It is difficult for us to take our big "suitcase" of cares and cast it over onto the Lord when we can't see Him. In the same way, it's difficult to take everything out of the messy, cluttered closets of our hearts and lay it all out before the Lord. It even takes awhile to get to the point where we *want* to clean out those overstuffed closets.

How do you get to that place? *You have to build faith in your heart until you believe without a shadow of a doubt that He is the answer.* The eyes of your spirit must "see" God as your only answer, for that is exactly what He is.

God Wants To Deliver You

You need to get the revelation that God not only has the capability and ability to do something about your situation, but He also *wants* to move on your behalf.

> **The Lord is my shepherd; I shall not want.**
>
> Psalm 23:1 *KJV*

> **Many are the afflictions of the righteous, but the Lord delivers him out of them all.**
>
> Psalm 34:17 *NKJV*

> **I will call upon the Lord, who is worthy to be praised: so shall I be saved from my enemies.**
>
> Psalm 18:3 *KJV*

> **The Lord will perfect that which concerns me; Your mercy, O Lord, endures forever; do not forsake the works of Your hands.**
>
> Psalm 138:8 *NKJV*

Notice that these verses say that *the Lord* delivers — *not* our mate or our best friend!

A wife might think, *I just need to tell my husband about this problem, and everything will be taken care of.* But that isn't how it works in God's Kingdom. Every time we look to man first rather than to our Heavenly Father, we diminish our ability to walk in faith.

Let's look again at First Peter 5:8. This scripture contains an awesome truth that you should meditate on, because it tells you the reason *why* you can cast your cares on God: He is absolutely head over heels in love with you! *Nothing* is too difficult for God, and He loves you enough to do the impossible in your life as you put your trust in Him.

EntrustYour Case
To The Specialist

You need to continually remind yourself how capable God really is to handle *all* of your life issues. He is not just a general practitioner. God is a Specialist who specializes in your cares.

So go ahead and leave all those other people out of the loop, and take the cares that have been weighing heavy on your heart straight to the Specialist! Turn loose of *all* your cares and worries, and leave them once and for all in God's capable hands. In Him is all the wisdom that there ever was. He knows *exactly* what to do and how to do it, and He will guide you every step of the way out of the problem and into peace.

Build Your House
With God's Wisdom

Proverbs 9:1 says that wisdom is a house-builder. That means we are building an eternal structure in our lives as we walk through each day. We're not just putting plaster on a hole in the wall. Everything we do in this life is for a greater purpose. There is more to this form of prayer we're talking about than just releasing some personal cares. It is all part of building our house with *wisdom*.

Learning the skill of casting your cares on the Lord will help you build your house with wisdom. With every situation that you entrust first to God, you will build your house a little bigger and a little stronger in Him.

Don't let it be said of you that in every situation of life, you immediately start looking for someone's phone number to call. Casting your cares on other people places you in a very precarious position in life, for they can never be the source of your answer.

No matter what the situation, learn to go first to God and His Word. Let the present challenge serve as an added building block in your spiritual house, fortifying your foundation with a new measure of God's wisdom. Always make sure that your *first* response is a *supernatural* response — one that places every detail of the matter squarely in the hands of the Lord.

CHAPTER 7

Don't Settle For a 'Pacifier'

Too often when we talk to a friend about our cares or about a situation we intend to pray for, we are "all talked out" by the time we have finished the conversation. Talking to another person pacifies the desire within us to pray, which consequently gets us out of the Spirit. This same thing also happens frequently when it comes to projects that the Holy Spirit has instructed us to work on.

Now, talking to another person about your cares or your projects from God and how you are going to pray about them can inspire you. There can be a place for that kind of conversation. And as the Bible says, there is safety in the counsel of many (Proverbs 11:14).

However, talking about your cares with another person, no matter how wise or capable that person is, will only pacify you. It will *not* satisfy your heart's desire to draw from the Source of wisdom Himself.

Don't *Pacify* Your Heart — *Satisfy* It

Just consider what happens when you give a pacifier to a baby. The pacifier soothes the baby because it makes him think he has something that he doesn't have.

In the same way, talking about your cares and worries with a friend or loved one will make you think you have done something you haven't done. You really haven't taken care of the problem. All you have done is relieve some pressure by casting your care over on your friend.

But what you want to do is *satisfy* your heart — not *pacify* it — by truly releasing all of the pressure. The only way to accomplish that goal is to cast your cares over on *God*.

This principle applies not only to your personal cares and anxieties, but also to your prayer assignments. For instance, if you start thinking about the scripture that says *all* mankind shall see the glory of God poured out (Isaiah 40:5), you can start feeling overwhelmed when you look around at "all mankind." That overwhelmed feeling can then begin to feel like a heavy burden

but you don't want to take on a burden when you pray. That is not God's plan. He is the only One who can do anything about such great matters, and He just wants you to be available to work with Him.

It's up to you. You can choose to stay up all night wringing your hands or talking to a friend, or you can pour out your heart to the Lord. However, if you don't learn how to truly cast your cares on the Lord, you will *not* be effective in other areas of prayer. Not only that, but you will also be worn out in the natural. Worry and stress will take their toll on your flesh, and you may eventually have to deal with sickness in your body on top of everything else.

Lead Others to the One Who Satisfies the Heart

Learn how to "hash things out" with your Father, for He is the Lover of your soul and a Friend who sticks closer than a brother. Once you have learned how to keep your mind free from cares and worries by releasing them to the Lord, you will then be in a position to truly help others.

You see, no matter how much you try to give someone counsel and advice from your own reservoir of knowledge and experience, God is the only One who has the needed wisdom, direction, and plan for that person's life. In fact, His plans and purposes for that individual were ordained before the foundation of the world.

True leadership in the Body of Christ is therefore demonstrated by the ability to lead people to the throne of God to get their needs met. We should never try to lead people to ourselves, nor should we allow them to use us to pacify their need to pray.

The best thing we can ever do for others is to point them to the Father and His Word. He alone is the One who can give them true rest from their worries so they can finally learn to live care-free.

CHAPTER 8

Living Care-Free

In Philippians 4:6-7, God gives us a firm command: *Do not worry.* In His eyes, our obedience to that command is not an option, but a *requirement.*

> **Do not fret or have any anxiety about anything, but in every circumstance and in everything, by prayer and petition (definite requests), with thanksgiving, continue to make your wants known to God.**
>
> **And God's peace [shall be yours, that tranquil state of a soul assured of its salvation through Christ, and so fearing nothing from God and being content with its earthly lot of whatever sort that is, that peace] which transcends all understanding shall garrison and mount guard over your hearts and minds in Christ Jesus.**

Worry is the exalting of the devil's opinion, your opinion, or someone else's opinion over *God's* opinion. It is having more faith in the devil's ability to harm you than in God's ability to deliver you. So when worry thoughts come to your mind, recognize that they are sent by the enemy to exalt themselves against the knowledge of God.

What is the knowledge of God in this matter? We see His knowledge revealed right here in Philippians 4:6: "...in every circumstance and in everything, by prayer and petition (definite requests), with thanksgiving, continue to make your wants known to God."

This is divine instruction about what to do when your mind is bombarded with negative thoughts such as:

- Your children are crazy! They're not going to ever be a success in life!
- You're not going to make it! This problem is too big to overcome.
- *You're sick, and you are going to die!*

Are these thoughts that originate in the knowledge of God? *No!* God has said something very specifically in His Word about these kinds of negative thoughts. He wants you to put thoughts like these *out* of your mind so you can put *in* His higher thoughts to replace them.

So what are you going to do the next time thoughts of worry and fear race through your mind about a situation you're facing in life? Call your friend? No, you're going to call God and tell Him all about it, just as you have done with your friends so many times in the past. Tell Him every detail. This is what you must do *first* if you are ever going to learn how to cast your cares on the Lord.

Take Off the Mask

One thing that will help you is to go to God and truly repent for the sin of worry. Tell Him, "Lord, I have worried. I have fretted. I have knots in my stomach. So right now I repent, Lord. I want to be healed so I can live care-free."

Don't be a hypocrite with God, trying to be all "pretty-sounding" by using words such as "Thee" and "Thou" when you address Him. Be honest and real with Him. Tell Him, "I feel terrible about this, Lord, because I have wasted so much time worrying instead of casting my care on You."

In past times, actors used white masks on a stick that expressed different emotions, such as happiness, sadness, or anger. The actor would put on the mask that represented the nature of the particular character he was portraying to the audience. "Hypocrite" means *one who speaks from behind the mask.* That definition should *not* describe you in your relationship with God. He knows you better than you know yourself, so don't go to Him speaking from behind your pretty mask. Be who you really are, since He already knows everything about you anyway.

When Jesus referred to people who are different on the inside from the way they are on the outside, He called them *hypocrites* — and, unfortunately, the modern Church has a host of different varieties!

So many masks exist in the Church today. Some people walk into church and leave their "world mask" on the coat rack with their coat and hat. Then as they walk into the sanctuary, they put on their "religious mask," which they wear the entire service. But the moment they walk out the church doors, they pull out their other mask and put it back on!

Most people have never learned to be real with their Heavenly Father. Then they wonder why people in the world say, "I don't want to go to church because there are so many hypocrites"!

Get In Position
To Minister Peace to Others

We need to learn to turn our hearts inside out with God. Then we can begin to live before the world as those who truly walk in divine love and abiding peace — and people *will* see the difference.

There is something unique about God's kind of peace. It stands out in this stressed-out world we live in. Most people can smell a fake a mile away, but they are drawn like moths to a flame to a person who truly abides in God's peace.

Have you ever prayed unsuccessfully for someone who was extremely upset? Perhaps you said a calm prayer and "spoke peace" over that person's soul — but after you finished, you could tell that nothing had transpired. The person might have given you a polite smile, but his eyes told the real story. The care and weight was still on him.

So maybe you got a little louder, a littler more forceful, and you *commanded* peace to come. But there is a problem with this method of ministering. *You* can't move the mountain! Mountains don't move in proportion to your level of force or loudness. It is God's hand alone that moves mountains. *Your role is to connect your faith with God's hand in order to release His power and His peace into a situation.*

As we learn to cast our cares on the Lord and walk in peace throughout our daily routine, we get ourselves in position to help others. On the other hand, if we spend all our time worrying and fretting about the circumstances we are facing, we are no help at all to someone who is desperate to receive the peace of God into his or her own situation.

Make it a priority to become skillful in walking in God's peace so you can help lead others down that same path. You are called to point people to the Word and to prayer, where they will find hope in God's promises, His power, and His love for them.

Whenever people start to pour out their problems to you, immediately direct them to the throne of God. Instruct them to share all the details of their situation with their Father who cares for them tenderly. That is how to help them get on the road to an abiding peace that surpasses understanding, no matter what may come their way.

The Divine Solution for Worry

Let's look at Philippians 4:6 again. It says, "Do not fret or have any anxiety about anything, but in every circumstance and in everything, *by prayer....*"

There it is — your only solution to every thought of worry that is tormenting your mind and weighing heavily on your heart: *"by prayer."* You won't be free of those cares until you give them to the One who can do something about them.

Tell God about the situation. Ask Him for His wisdom and His counsel. Make a definite request for the answer to your need based on His Word. Be honest before Him, and repent for allowing yourself to worry. Then from your heart, lift up specific petitions and requests, knowing that your Father loves you and is well able to give you what you need every time without fail.

Philippians 4:6 goes on to further explain the divine solution for worry: "...by prayer and petition (definite requests), *with thanksgiving....*" However, don't get the idea that this is a formula you can mechanically follow (i.e., *step 1:* prayer; *step 2:* specific petition; *step 3:* give thanks). Thanksgiving is a natural response from your heart, not an automatic, mechanical motion.

Think back to the earlier example of the dump truck. If someone came and drove a truckload of garbage off your property to dispose of it, your natural response would be to thank that person for his service. In the same way, praise and thanksgiving will begin to flow up out of your heart as you cast the weight of your cares on the Lord and experience a newfound sense of freedom and release.

The Role of Worship

If we go to a worship service before we have truly followed these steps, the worship can act like a spiritual sedative, making us feel like all is well. But when the service is over, the weight of our cares can come crashing back onto our souls — unless we finally, by prayer and definite petitions, cast those cares on the Lord and trust Him to take care of them.

Times of worship *can* be a good opportunity for us to bear our hearts before the Lord. However, this can only happen if we follow Jesus' command in John 4 to worship *in spirit and in truth*.

Don't waste time when you are in an anointed atmosphere. Get real with God. Tell Him truthfully where your heart is and what is weighing heavily on you. Repent for allowing worry and fear to occupy your soul, keeping you from your primary call — to live before Him. Tell God *everything*. Then make your requests to Him, and with thanksgiving, from your heart begin to receive His wisdom and grace. Acknowledge that He is the only answer to your cares.

As you do this, verse 7 will become a reality, and just as the old song says there will be: "*Peace, peace, wonderful peace, flowing down from the Father above.*" Wherever anxiety, care, fear, and worry are absent, peace is manifested. The death of sin and worry is swallowed up in life — the life found in the Word and in God's presence. An exchange has taken place — your cares exchanged for His peace.

Maintaining the Walk of Peace

Peace actually serves as a spiritual weapon. The text says that peace *mounts guard* over your heart and mind. Peace is like an outstretched arm that sends the message to fear and worry: *"No, you can't come back in here."* Peace is an attribute of the Kingdom of Heaven, and its presence in our lives is proof that we are submitted under the mighty hand of God.

But once peace comes, how do we maintain it? Verse 8 tells us:

> **Finally, brethren, whatsoever things are true, whatsoever things are honest, whatsoever things are just, whatsoever things are pure, whatsoever things are lovely, whatsoever things are of good report; if there be any virtue, and if there be any praise, think on these things.**

We maintain our peace by keeping our minds filled with the Word of God. Continually meditating on what God has promised us concerning particular situations in our lives, will cause us to stay free from cares and worries and keep our faith strong until we see the fullness of what we are believing Him for.

Conclusion

To summarize, remember to always keep first things first in prayer. You can't be used effectively to pray for nations until you learn how to cast your own cares onto God.

Meditate on the Word regarding how much God loves you and how mighty His hand is to deliver you. Then talk to Him as you would your closest friend.

Drop the religious mask, and be honest before your Father. Make your specific requests, then receive from Him with a heart of thanksgiving.

Never let a day go by without cleaning off your spiritual shelves of all cares and worries. Throw all of the contents on your Heavenly Father, knowing that He tenderly cares for you.

Above all, keep your mind full of the Word. This is the key that will keep you steady on your course toward enjoying a carefree life before God. As you do all of these things, you will find that the peace that passes all understanding will become an abiding reality in your life.

HOW TO COME TO GOD-LET HIM WHO THIRSTS COME

Introduction

When you received Jesus as your Savior, you were given the power to become a son of God (John 1:12). As a son, there is one thing you can know for certain — you can *always* come to the Father. He has made a way for you to come to Him through His Son Jesus.

To live life on this earth as a son, you will have to come to God on a continual basis. The further you move away from Him, the further you move away from the benefits of sonship.

The Bible commands us to be imitators of the Father (Ephesians 5:1). We don't have to encourage our children to imitate us; they do that as a natural part of spending time with us. As sons of God, we must do the same. We must continually come to Him and do all that He asks us to do to stay close to Him.

These are the truths we will discuss in this book.

Lucy McKee

CHAPTER 1

Jesus' Work Was Sufficient

We approach God not because of what we've done or based on our own works. We approach Him *based on what Jesus did for us*. Jesus didn't willingly lay down His life for us just so we can go to Heaven when we die. His work of redemption affects every part of our lives here on this earth as well. Jesus made it possible for us to be sons — and as sons, we can come freely into the presence of our Father.

Think of all Jesus did to purchase our redemption for us. Preceding the Cross, the flogging He endured purchased our complete *physical* healing. The crown of thorns that the soldiers pushed onto Jesus' head purchased our total wholeness *mentally*. And this was all *before the Cross!*

Then on the Cross, Jesus took our sin upon Himself, making us righteous before God and giving us back the authority and dominion Adam had lost through sin. Jesus made it possible for us to be prosperous in every realm of our lives — spiritually, mentally, physically, materially, and socially. He was made poor so we could be rich (2 Corinthians 8:9). His death and resurrection opened the way for the Holy Spirit to come and live within us. This is why our full identity with Jesus' work of redemption necessarily leads to *a new and glorious life to be lived before God*.

Nothing Can Be Added
to What Jesus Has Already Done

Do you have any problems? Through Jesus' death, burial, and resurrection, He gave you the ability to overcome in every situation. If His redemptive work hasn't yet affected every single area of your life, it *will* as you determine to draw near to the Heavenly Father.

The Bible says that if you receive Jesus, God gives you the power to become His son. Jesus' life manifested through you can then affect every life you touch — but only after the power of His life first transforms your own. The purpose of sonship is not to allow you to look back on Jesus' life only when you go to church or take Communion. Rather, it is to give you the ability to live His life every single day as a son of God.

But realize this: The life Jesus gave us can diminish if we begin to walk through our days in our own power and ability. This diminishing will occur whenever we try to add on to what Jesus did. That's what is called *walking according to the flesh.*

Jesus' Blood Is Enough

I remember a particular time I had sinned. I had made this same mistake before, so I went before the Lord and I said, "I'm so sorry, Father. I'm *so* sorry. I'll tell You what I'll do — I'll fast. I won't even eat a thing." Then I began to add other things I'd do to make up for my sin. "Lord, I also won't talk to anyone. [My husband can testify to the big sacrifice *that* would have been for me!] I'll just read the Word all day and listen to You."

I continued saying how *dreadfully* sorry I was. I went on and on, and somehow I really thought I was ministering to the Lord with all the sacrifices I was willing to make. Ideas from my own fleshly mind just kept coming to me of what I could do.

Finally, I got quiet in my heart and began to listen for the Lord's voice — and this is what He said: "*So the blood of My Son, which He shed to pay for this sin, is not enough for you? Does more blood need to be shed just for you?*"

The Lord continued, "*There isn't anything you can add to what My Son did for you. You've asked forgiveness so where's your faith? Your task right*

108

now is to believe in faith that My blood has cleansed you from your sin. Apply that blood to the doorposts of your heart and mind; then get up and be a doer of what you tell others to do!"

Sometimes we think we're being so spiritual by trying to help God along. But that is precisely the wrong way to think! God's work on the Cross was *good* enough, *strong* enough, and *special* enough! There is nothing so extreme we've ever done or will ever do that Jesus' blood did not cover — past, present, and future.

Every time you miss it — every single time you make a mistake you've made before — Jesus' blood is there. When the Father looks at you, He doesn't see all the flaws and failures you think He sees. He sees you cleansed by the blood of His Son. That means you can come into the Father's presence anytime you want to as a son made righteous in Christ.

CHAPTER 2

When Do We Come to Jesus?

The first time we came to Jesus was the moment we got saved. Regardless of our different lives and backgrounds, all of us came with everything we had. Whatever we were, whoever we were, we came to be born again, not of flesh but of the Spirit (John 3:5).

You may have first come to Jesus by someone else's invitation. Someone may have said to you, "Come to church." Or you may have heard a pastor say, "Come forward, and come to Jesus."

But no matter what any person may have said, there was something on the inside of you that drew you to Jesus. You may have heard someone else's audible words, but the Spirit of God Himself came and began to draw your heart to your Savior (John 6:44). The Father did that for you, the same way He did it for each of us when we initially came to Christ.

We Come To Know Him Personally

In John 4, we read of certain Samaritans who came to Jesus for the first time. These people were introduced to the Master after He spoke with one woman at a well. When that woman realized she was speaking with the Messiah, she ran to tell her neighbors.

"Come, see a Man who told me all things that I ever did. Could this be the Christ?" Then they went out of the city and came to Him.

John 4:29,30 *NKJV*

John says that many Samaritans believed in Him simply by hearing the testimony of the woman. But many others were convinced only after they went to Him themselves.

And they told the woman, "Now we no longer believe (trust, have faith) just because of what you said; for we have heard Him ourselves — personally; and we know that He truly is the Savior of the world, the Christ."

John 4:42

After the Samaritans heard Jesus speak, they said to the woman, "Now we believe this Man — not because of what you said, but because *we* have heard Him. Now we know Him personally ourselves."

It's the same way when you meet a new person. When you hear about someone you've never met, it helps you "know" that person to some extent. But when you meet that individual for yourself, you begin to know him or her personally.

Each of us must enter into a personal relationship with Jesus as well. We've been born again, and He has become our Lord. We no longer have to come to Him by a person's invitation. We come now because we have a personal testimony about how God saved *us*.

It's a Process

Now that we've entered into that personal relationship with Jesus, the apostle Peter explains that God wants us to *keep* drawing near.

Like newborn babies you should crave (thirst for, earnestly desire) the pure (unadulterated) spiritual milk, that by it you may be nurtured and grow unto [completed] salvation, since you have [already] tasted the goodness and kindness of the Lord.

COME TO HIM [then, to that] Living Stone which men tried and threw away, but which is chosen [and] precious in God's sight. [Come] and, like living stones, be yourselves built [into] a spiritual house, for a holy (dedicated, consecrated) priesthood, to offer up [those] spiritual sacrifices [that are] acceptable and pleasing to God through Jesus Christ.

1 Peter 2:2-5

The Bible plainly says in verse 4, "*Come* to Him." It *doesn't* say, "When you *came* to Him...." It isn't talking about being born again. It's talking to those of us who have "...[already] tasted the goodness and kindness of the Lord" (v. 3). Verse 5 goes on to say, "[Come] and, like living stones, be yourselves built [into] a spiritual house, for a holy (dedicated, consecrated) priesthood...."

In other words, we come to one Person — the chosen, honored, precious Chief Cornerstone, Jesus. But our coming to this precious Living Stone is not a one-time spiritual action; it is a continual *process*. We are always coming to Him, that we may be built into a spiritual house and a holy priesthood that brings glory to Him.

CHAPTER 3

He Calls Continually

Jesus has given us an open invitation to come into His presence and draw our life from Him. He spoke of this continual process of coming to Him in John 6:35 (*NKJV*):

Jesus replied, "I am the Bread of Life. He who comes to Me will never be hungry, and he who believes on and cleaves to and trusts in and relies on Me will never thirst any more — at any time."

Jesus called Himself the Bread of Life. In other words, if you're going to have life, you must have intimate contact with the Bread of Life, for only he who *comes* to Jesus will cease to be hungry.

Notice that there is no promise in God's Word for the person who does *not* come. Jesus is able to do what He has promised for the one who *comes* to Him.

Jesus went on to say in John 6:37 (*NKJV*) that if you do come to Him, He will never reject you: "All that the Father gives Me will come to Me, and the one who comes to Me I will by no means cast out." Jesus will never say to you, "Get away from Me, you sorry person!" No, He is always saying, "If you come to Me, I will *never* cast you out."

The Holy Spirit Never Stops
Drawing You to the Father

Then Jesus says in verse 44 (*NKJV*), "No one can come to Me unless the Father who sent Me draws him; and I will raise him up at the last day." No matter what circumstances surrounded your decision to come to Jesus the first time to accept Him as your Savior, you can be assured of this: It was the Spirit of God Himself who came to you and began to draw you to the Father through His Son.

However, it isn't God's intent to draw you to Him only one time. The Holy Spirit's call within your heart, bidding you to come into the Father's presence, is a daily process. Always the Holy Spirit is drawing you toward the Father, calling you to spend time in intimate fellowship with Him.

Sometimes the Holy Spirit calls me many times during the course of a day, and I'm too busy to pick up on it. By the end of the day, I find myself agitated, and I don't know why. I start asking myself, *Okay, what is it? Why am I feeling bothered on the inside? Is it something to do with the house? The food? The children?*

Finally, I just stop and resign myself to doing nothing else until I understand what's going on. I ask the Lord, "What is it? Why do I feel this way?" That's when I find out He's been calling me all day long, and I haven't been listening!

Sometimes that's how we have to come. The Holy Spirit calls us all day long until we finally stop long enough to pay attention to His still, small voice and say, "Okay, Lord. I'll stop all my busyness and spend time with You."

No, it isn't God's intention to draw you once in a while. The Holy Spirit *ever* abides within you, calling you to come.

Spiritual Thirst Is Quenched
In His Presence

In John 7:37 (*NKJV*), Jesus said, "... If anyone thirsts, let him come to Me and drink." Literal water isn't going to satisfy this kind of thirst. Man's spiritual thirst is quenched when he comes to Jesus and drinks his fill of His presence. As a result, Jesus promised, "...out of his heart will flow rivers of living water. But this He spoke concerning the Spirit..." (v. 38).

We see the culmination of this divine invitation in Revelation 22:17 (*NKJV*) — almost the last verse in the entire Bible.

> **And the Spirit and the bride say, "Come!" And let him who hears say, "Come!" And let him who thirsts come. Whoever desires, let him take the water of life freely.**

This is the Father's grand invitation to all who will listen: "The Spirit and the bride invite you to *come*. Anyone who thirsts, *come* and drink freely of My abundant and eternal life."

CHAPTER 4

Come to the Living Word

We have established that as sons of God, we are to experience a continual coming to Jesus. But note what Jesus said to a group of religious Jews:

> And the Father Who sent Me has Himself testified concerning Me. Not one of you has ever given ear to His voice or seen His form (His face — what He is like). [You have always been deaf to His voice and blind to the vision of Him.] And you have not His word (His thought) living in your hearts, because you do not believe and adhere to and trust in and rely on Him Whom He has sent. [That is why you do not keep His message living in you, because you do not believe in the Messenger Whom He has sent.]
>
> You search and investigate and pore over the Scriptures diligently, because you suppose and trust that you have eternal life through them. And these [very Scriptures] testify about Me! And still you are not willing [but refuse] to come to Me, so that you might have life.
>
> John 5:37-39

Verse 39 tells us something profound. *We don't obtain life from the Scriptures, but from coming to Jesus Himself.*

Jesus was talking to leading Jewish leaders and theologians when He spoke those words in John 5. Many of these people had memorized the entire the Word of God, which at that time would have included the Law and the Prophets. They had spent much of their lives studying the Scriptures to find out everything they could about the coming Messiah. Yet when that very Messiah was standing in front of them, they refused to come to Him and receive His saving power.

So we see that Jesus is able to save those who come to Him. This truth applies not only to the first moment of salvation, but also to every subsequent moment in our walk with God. Our coming to Jesus must be a continual act of obedience, something we do over and over again as naturally as we breathe. We are not walking through this life all alone. But Jesus said that *those who come to Him* are the ones He is able to help.

Go to Your Savior
For The Help You Need

Jesus rebuked those Jewish leaders because they totally misunderstood the purpose of God's Word. Jesus' message to us today is similar: "You're trying to create your world using the Scriptures — but in doing so, you have made Me unnecessary."

Let me give you an example. I'm thinking of a businessman I know who has an unusually strong call on his life as a giver. At one point, he was helping so many people that his right hand didn't even know what his left hand was doing (Matthew 6:3)!

But then several setbacks occurred all at once, and this man's business and financial holdings began to crash all around him. So he stepped up his level of confessing scriptures, praying, reading good Christian books, and listening to teaching CDs in order to keep his faith level high. He *came to* the Word; he *came to* those books; he *came to* those teaching series, and he really got inspired.

But something was wrong. The businessman had a good heart and was doing everything he knew to do, yet things were getting worse and worse. He thought, *What's the deal here? What am I doing wrong?*

The man was deeply concerned about the potential fallout of this situation. Because of his obedience to the vision God had planted in his heart years ago, hundreds of people were now depending on him for their livelihood. He knew he couldn't just give up and say to all those people, "Sorry about that — hope you have a good life!"

So the man came to me for counsel. After he explained the situation to me and described all the things he'd been doing to receive guidance and build up his faith, I told him, "Listen, you have to go to Jesus and ask *Him* what to do. Set aside time to be alone with Him, and take a pen and pad of paper with you. Write down everything He speaks to your heart just for today. *Go to the Savior.*"

This businessman took my words to heart and began to set aside time to get alone with Jesus. Every day he wrote down what the Holy Spirit told him to do, and every day the Lord gave him a specific plan for that day. For instance, one day the Holy Spirit might tell him, "I want you to move those funds over here" or "Today I want you to go talk to this person." And because this man made the decision to come to Jesus every day, Jesus took his hand and walked him out of the crisis, step by step.

The Holy Spirit Will Reveal
The Truth You Need for Victory

Let me share one of the passages of Scripture I gave this businessman when he first came to talk with me. I wanted to help him understand *how* God was going to deliver him from that situation.

> But when He, the Spirit of Truth (the Truth-giving Spirit) comes, He will guide you into all the Truth (the whole, full Truth). For He will not speak His own message [on His own authority]; but He will tell whatever He hears [from the Father; He will give the message that has been given to Him], and He will announce and declare to you the things that are to come [that will happen in the future].
>
> He will honor and glorify Me, because He will take of (receive, draw upon) what is Mine and will reveal (declare, disclose, transmit) it to you.

John 16:13,14

The Holy Spirit will take the things that are of Jesus and will reveal them to you. That means the Holy Spirit is going to help you see truth clearly. He will disclose certain keys to release victory into a situation that you couldn't possibly know otherwise. He will make a way for you to understand what you need to understand.

Like a divine transmitter, the Holy Spirit will give you the truth you need syllable by syllable, if that's the way you can best receive it. You can depend on Him to faithfully take hold of your hand, just as He did that businessman, and walk you out of any difficult situation you are facing.

You see, "saving" isn't Jesus' hobby or side job; it's His primary job description. A savior is one who is disposed to and particularly good at the task of saving — and the Bible tells us that Jesus is *the* Savior. Saving is a skill that comes naturally to Him!

So plant this truth deep in your heart: After Jesus initially saved you the first time you came to Him, He didn't stop being your Savior. He is *always* your Savior. Every day He knows exactly what you need and what you need to be saved from — and He always knows it *ahead of time*. Jesus *will* save you — *if* you will come to Him. He'll give you a specific plan that will lead you victoriously through every situation you're about to encounter, even before you know what those situations are.

CHAPTER 5

Jesus Will Again Deliver Us!

Notice what Paul said to the Corinthian church about Jesus' role as Savior and Deliverer in our lives:

> [For it is He] Who rescued and saved us from such a perilous death, and He will still rescue and save us; in and on Him we have set our hope (our joyful and confident expectation) that He will again deliver us [from danger and destruction and draw us to Himself],

> 2 Corinthians 1:10

Jesus *will again* deliver us. This means that whether we're attacked by the enemy or if adverse circumstances arise or we get ourselves in a mess, Jesus stands ready to deliver us as we come to Him for help.

Jesus Is Our Only Deliverer

When our own past mistakes create problems in our lives, we sometimes imagine our Heavenly Father saying to us, "You got yourself into this mess; now you can get yourself out of it." The truth is, we as parents may have said those very words to our children at one time or another. But our Father doesn't say that to us when we come to Him for help.

123

He sent His Son Jesus to be our Savior — and Jesus is in the business of saving us to the uttermost!

> **Therefore He [Jesus] is also ABLE TO SAVE TO THE UTTERMOST THOSE WHO COME TO GOD THROUGH HIM, since He always lives to make intercession for them.**
>
> **Hebrews 7:25** *NKJV*

When we accepted Jesus as our Savior, we didn't instantaneously change and become mature. And since that day when we first came to Him, not one of us has become so mature that we can now begin to go to *ourselves* for the answers to the problems we face in life. No! In our Christian walk, the Source of our deliverance will never change. It is "one-stop shopping" at the feet of Jesus, because He has every answer we could ever need.

Apart From The Source Of Life, We Have No Life

Jesus said to the Jewish leaders in John 5:39, "You search the Scriptures, for in them you think you have eternal life; and these are they which testify of Me. But you are not willing to *come to Me that you may have life.*"

If we are to live as sons of God on this earth and allow God's work to have its perfect work in our lives, we cannot live apart from Jesus. We must come to the Source of life.

The Word is not to be put in practice apart from Jesus. The Word is a mirror, and as we diligently look into that mirror, we will begin to see Jesus' reflection on *us*. But God's Word is not going to do a work in our lives on its own. It only works in connection with our coming to Jesus, the One who has delivered us and will continue to deliver us in every situation.

CHAPTER 6

A New and Living Way
To God

In Hebrews 10, we find a divine invitation extended to us *to come forward* and *draw near* to the Father's throne:

> Therefore, brethren, since we have full freedom and confidence to enter into the [Holy of] Holies [by the power and virtue] in the blood of Jesus, by THIS FRESH (NEW) AND LIVING WAY which He initiated and dedicated and opened for us through the separating curtain (veil of the Holy of Holies), that is, through His flesh, and since we have [such] a great and wonderful and noble Priest [Who rules] over the house of God.
>
> LET US ALL COME FORWARD AND DRAW NEAR with true (honest and sincere) hearts in unqualified assurance and absolute conviction engendered by faith (by that leaning of the entire human personality on God in absolute trust and confidence in His power, wisdom, and goodness), having our hearts sprinkled and purified from a guilty (evil) conscience and our bodies cleansed with pure water.
>
> Hebrews 10:19-21

If we are walking in obedience to God, we are always moving forward *toward Him*. As we draw near to God with true, honest, and sincere hearts, He always causes us to move forward. We cannot remain as we are.

Now, it may take awhile for your circumstances to change, but when you start coming to God on a daily basis, you immediately begin to build strength in your heart. You move forward with a new sense of confidence and trust in the Lord's faithfulness to uphold you. You're no longer bowed down in depression because of the storms of life still swirling around you.

Intimacy — Or Religious Duty?

Consider your own relationship with God. Are you continually moving forward? Or has your relationship with the Father gradually changed from a daily walk of vital intimacy to a series of religious duties in which you just go through the motions? If so, you're in danger of losing a sense of Jesus' living presence in your life.

If you're wondering whether or not you've gotten religious in your spiritual walk, compare yourself to Jesus' description of the Jews who engaged in dead religion:

> **You search the Scriptures, for in them you think you have eternal life; and these are they which testify of Me. But you are not willing to come to Me that you may have life.**
>
> **John 5:39,40 NKJV**

These were people who knew the Scriptures but weren't willing to personally come to Jesus to experience His life.

People who fit this category today may continue to go to church and do whatever is necessary to make them look like good Christians. But they have a problem: They're not really making it to *Jesus*.

This is a tragedy, since Jesus provided for us a new and living way through His precious blood (Hebrews 10:20). It is a way that gives us access to the very throne room of God. All we have to do is choose to *come* to Him.

Building a Strong Foundation

Jesus promised, "Come to Me, all you who labor and are heavy-laden and overburdened, and I will cause you to rest. [I will ease and relieve and refresh your souls]" (Matthew 11:28). Jesus takes it very personally when you come to Him. He says, "I've provided a way for you to come to me whenever you want. And when you come, I will give you whatever it is you need."

In Luke 6:47 (*NKJV*), Jesus related a parable that reveals the divine order of steps we are to take in order to build a solid foundation in our lives. He said, "Whoever *comes* to Me, and *hears* My sayings and *does* them, I will show you whom he is like."

Then Jesus went on to describe a man who built his house on a rock, able to withstand the wind and storms. But notice the vital first step in building a strong foundation in our lives: We must first *come* to Jesus.

CHAPTER 7

Come to the Author Of Your Faith

We are called to come to Jesus in every situation — even when we think we already know what He will tell us.

Sometimes we think we know certain truths in the Word because we studied those scriptures at one time. We even underlined the verses in our Bible! So regarding those particular truths, we assume we really don't need to come to Jesus to receive understanding and wisdom. After all, we already know what to do! We think, *I know what God has promised me, so now it's just a matter of my putting that promise into practice. I just need to quote the Word.*

But would that be the right attitude for us to adopt in that situation? No! That negates the necessity of our coming to the Savior to spend time in His presence. And if we don't come to Jesus, we won't hear what He wants to say to us specifically about the matter we're facing at that moment. The written Word of God is *never* to replace *the Living Word.*

Jesus Will Throw You a Lifeline
When You Come To Him

I remember one time when I was really worrying about a certain matter — even though I know the Word, preach the Word, study the Word, read the Word, and virtually *live* in the Word! But that night I couldn't sleep, so I went upstairs to my desk in the middle of the night and prayed, "Help me, Lord. I know worry is a sin, but I'm worried about this situation." (Sometimes the most spiritual prayer we can pray is *"Help me!"*)

I opened the Word of God and did what my sister Lynne calls a "flop and stop." Now, this is not a method of Bible study that I'd recommend to you. Usually when we open the Bible at random, expecting to receive a word from the Lord, we land on some obscure passage like the genealogies of Christ!

However, this was one of those times when the method actually worked. I opened the Bible, and my eyes landed on a verse I'd studied before. It was already underlined and highlighted in my Bible. I may have even preached on that verse. But even though I'd seen that verse before, this time was different. I saw it right after coming to Jesus and praying, *"Help me, Lord."* So this time when I saw that verse, *the truth it contained became Jesus to me in that moment.*

I grabbed that promise in my heart, and I thanked God for performing it on my behalf. I had come to Jesus, and He had given me that word. I knew He was going to watch over that word to perform it.

That verse became my lifeline in the situation I was facing as I put it into practice. Every time a thought would come to my mind about the matter I'd been worrying about, I held on to that promise, replacing the thoughts of worry with the truth of that verse.

Trust the Author of Your Faith

In every situation, Jesus will both author and finish your faith — *if* you will come to Him. He is personally the Author of your faith in every situation.

When we don't go to our Savior for everything we need, it automatically becomes our responsibility to make God's Word work for us. But our part is to come to Jesus, believing "...that He is, and that He is a rewarder of those who diligently seek Him" (Hebrews 11:6).

Notice that this scripture *doesn't* say, "believe the *Word*," although we certainly must feed on the written Word in our daily lives. But it is the living Word — Jesus Himself — who is the Author and the Finisher of our faith in every single situation of our lives (Hebrews 12:2).

I found this to be true in that situation I was so worried about. *I came to Jesus, and He authored my faith for a favorable outcome.*

When I first talked to Him about the matter, I said, "Lord, You know that I know how to stand in faith, but I know that right now, I am *not* in faith. (It's a good thing to be honest with the Lord. He knows anyway, so you may as well just tell Him when you're not in faith!) Since Your Word says You are the Author of my faith, I need you to author faith for me right now. Please give me what I need to help me hold fast to Your Word regarding this situation."

Jesus answered that prayer by giving me a particular scripture as my lifeline. And in the end, He was faithful to perform His promise. I came through the entire situation with a strong sense of God's loving hand guiding me to victory every step of the way.

The Consequences
Of *Not* Coming to Jesus

However, there have been other situations in my life where I *didn't* come to Jesus — and they didn't turn out so well. I thought I knew enough to handle those challenges. Although I never made a conscious decision to leave Jesus out of the equation, my heart attitude was, "Lord, I don't need any help with this one. I know the scriptures to stand on. So thanks for wanting to help me, but I'll catch You on the flip side of the situation." In essence, I was telling Jesus that, at least in these cases, I didn't need Him to be the Author of my faith.

The Bible says that God gives understanding to the *simple* (Psalm 119:130). So what does He do for smart people who think they can figure out everything on their own? The answer is — *not much.*

God can't do hardly anything for us when we think we don't need Him. Knowledge never replaces the blessed Savior. In fact, knowledge puffs us up like a big, deployed airbag (1 Corinthians 8:1)!

So before you set out to take a mountain by faith, come to Jesus. As you spend time with Him in prayer and worship, He will edify you, give you the wisdom you need to know which way to go, and strengthen you to finish the task. You won't be on your own any longer, straining and pushing as you try to perform and produce results.

Just come boldly before the Throne of Grace, God's place of favor. There you will find the Author and Finisher of your faith waiting for you. And as you draw near to Him, He will provide abundant mercy and all the grace you need to help you in your time of need (Hebrews 4:16).

CHAPTER 8

Utter Dependency
Equals Spiritual Maturity

In the natural growing process of a child, the goal of good parents is to raise that child and help him mature so he can ultimately leave home and live independently as a productive adult. Parents want their children to grow up to become independent and launch out on their own. That's the normal and healthy process of natural maturation.

But in the Kingdom of God, it's totally opposite. If you think you can go through life without much help from God, you aren't spiritually mature at all. The real key to maturity in God is the realization that you need Him in every area of your life more than you've ever needed anything before!

When Christians have the attitude, "I've got this situation covered; I can handle it on my own," do you know what that attitude reveals? Immaturity. That's the way spiritually immature people think.

Maturity in God results in the realization that you can't live from one minute to the next without Him. You need Him every minute in order to do what He's called you to do. You feel the responsibility of the task, so you go to Him continually, asking for His strength and wisdom. Believe me, the more you grow in God, the more you know you are *not* independent; in fact, you are *totally* dependent on Him.

Jesus was the mature Son of God, the perfect Example for all of us who are called to live as grown-up sons of God. Yet Jesus declared, "…

The Son can do nothing of Himself, but what He sees the Father do; for whatever He does, the Son also does in like manner" (John 5:19 *NKJV*). Later Jesus said it again: "I can of Myself do nothing. As I hear, I judge; and My judgment is righteous, because I do not seek My own will but the will of the Father who sent Me" (John 5:30 *NKJV*).

Was Jesus lying when He spoke those words? Was He just telling a story? No, absolutely not. Jesus always came *to* the Father before He did anything *for* the Father.

Live Your Life Connected to Jesus

According to Jesus, your Christian life is not to be lived apart from Him:

> **I am the vine, you are the branches. He who abides in Me, and I in him, bears much fruit; for without Me you can do nothing.**
>
> **John 15:5** *NKJV*

Jesus died for you so you could know the perpetual motion of coming to Him on a continual basis and living in His Presence. You are not to come to Him only on Sunday mornings at church or at the mid-week prayer meeting. Your life is to be lived *in Him* and *with Him*.

Jesus knows everything you're doing, and He has something to say about every single part of your life — your coworkers, your employees, your church, your home life, your friends, your personal habits, where you go, and what you do with your time. He'll even tell you what to say to the devil!

In every situation of life, remember this: Jesus will be the Author and Finisher of your faith when you come to Him. No matter how difficult the challenge you face, He is your Savior, your Deliverer, your Helper, and your Advocate.

It is true that apart from Jesus, you can do nothing. However, it is also true that when you come to Jesus to receive grace and mercy in time of need, He will do exceedingly more than you could ever ask or imagine, and *nothing* will be impossible to you!

CHAPTER 9

Go To The Source

Prayer is one way to come to God; however, it's possible to start praying and never even acknowledge that you're coming to Him. I know that because I've been guilty of doing it!

For instance, there have been times when I've started my prayer time by confessing scriptures strictly from my head and not my heart. I may have sounded good as I declared, "God has not given me a spirit of fear but of love and of power and a sound mind. I know I'm the head and not the tail." But because I hadn't taken the time to come into God's presence and acknowledge Him first, my words had no power behind them.

As Close as Your Next Breath

The truth is, even though confessing God's Word is a scriptural thing to do, we need to come to Jesus first and find out what He wants us to do in a particular situation. The first step should always be to acknowledge His Lordship in our lives and wait in His presence. Only then will we be ready to receive His guidance and do what He tells us to do.

There may be certain people or situations on your heart that you want to ask God about. You can pray, "Father, I need You to give me a scripture to hold on to. I need a scripture to become my lifeline. I need

You to save me in the midst of this situation, Jesus. Please tell me what I need to do."

Remember what the apostle Paul said: "…It is no longer I who live, but Christ lives in me…" (Galatians 2:20 *NKJV*). Jesus is living in you in the Person of the Holy Spirit. He's as close as your next breath.

Stay Close To the 'Input' End Of Your Spiritual Walk

Second Corinthians 5:15 (*NKJV*) says, "He [Jesus] died for all, that those who live should live no longer for themselves, but for Him who died for them and rose again." We are called to live for Jesus. However, our first ministry is come *to* Him. If we never get around to coming *to* Jesus, we're never going to do all we're called to do *for* Him.

Recently the Lord gave me a good illustration of this truth while I was standing in my garden on a very hot day. That day I was *not* a happy camper. We'd just returned from a trip, and all the plants were looking sad, wilted, and dry. *Everything* needed a good watering — but I was in a hurry because I had a lot of other things I needed to do.

So I got out the hose and pulled it around the corner, walking over to some droopy potted plants that looked particularly bad. But as I pointed the nozzle toward the plants, only a trickle of water dribbled out. Because I was in a hurry, I thought, *I do NOT want to take the time to walk all the way back to that faucet! I'll just pull the hose tight and let gravity help the water start flowing.* So I tried that — but it didn't work. Only a dribble of water was still coming out of the nozzle.

Then I gave the hose a jerk and started turning it every which way to make the water come out. That didn't work either. *Nothing* worked until I finally gave in and walked all the way back to the source of the problem — and found out that the hose had a kink in it.

As long as I stayed down at the "outflow" end of the hose, I couldn't fix my problem. But as soon as I decided to make the effort to go all the way back to the "input" end, I found the hindrance and dealt with it — and water began to flow freely again.

Notice that I didn't have to say or do a lot of complicated things to the hose to cause the water to come out. I just had to go back to the source and make sure the connection was no longer blocked. Once I got the kink out of the hose, I just stood there holding it as the water effortlessly flowed out and watered the plants. I was no longer pushing or agonizing or trying hard the way I did before. Now the water just came out on its own because I had taken care of the hindrance at the source.

This same principle applies to the Body of Christ. So often we stay at the "output" end of our walk with God, always trying to produce more and perform better in our own strength. But in reality, we don't need any more of our own efforts; the one thing we need is *more of Jesus.*

We need to come back to our Source — the "input" end of our spiritual walk — and receive a continual, fresh flow of the river of life that flows forth from Jesus. Without the life-giving inflow of His strength and grace, we will produce very little of worth, no matter how much we push and strain in our own efforts.

Come to the Source
and Receive *Life*

I remember a time when God really drove this particular truth home to my heart. It happened during a trip to Israel with a team of fellow Christians. We traveled to Mount Hermon, which is the water source both for Israel and for the surrounding nations. We noticed that the water flowing from the high slopes of Mount Hermon was very clear and fresh. Standing next to one of the streams flowing down from the mountain, we could see through the clean, transparent water to the rocks on the stream bottom. These fresh waters of Mount Hermon flow down the mountain in a multitude of streams and brooks, providing water for all of Israel's villages.

We climbed back on our bus and continued to travel south. Later our guide pointed to a river and said, "Look! There is some of the water that came down from Mount Hermon!"

It was unbelievable. Everyone in our group wanted to exclaim, "No, it couldn't be! That water is gross!"

Nearby was a spot where many people enjoyed picnics along the bank of the river. But the water was dirty, mixed with human waste and garbage. It looked *nothing* like the water we had seen flowing down from the top of Mount Hermon!

The truth is, the original source of Israel's water wasn't even Mount Hermon — it was the snow and rain that fell from the skies onto the mountain. And the further we traveled away from that original source where the precipitation first came down to water the earth, the more foul the water became.

This experience really taught me something about the state of the Church today. I've often asked myself, *How is the Church going to find her supernatural edge in this day? Who can provide the glory we are longing for?* There is only one answer to those questions. We must come to Jesus!

We have to stop spending all our own energy trying to "get out the kinks" that hinder the flow of God's Spirit in our midst. *We just need to continually come to our Source and receive the life-giving waters that flow freely and continually from His presence!*

That's what sons do. They come to their father when they need provision, guidance, wisdom, or strength. If *we* want to live our lives on this earth as spiritual sons, we, too, must choose to come to our Heavenly Father. He never ceases to call us, and there is never a time when we should not heed His call. We must continually keep coming to our Source of all life until the final trumpet blows and we see Jesus in all His glory.

HOW TO WALK
WITH GOD AND
FULFILL YOUR DESTINY

Introduction

God has a plan and purpose for your life. The Bible tells us that this plan and purpose has been designed since the foundation of the world, including His plan to redeem us. First Peter 1:18-20 says,

> "You must know (recognize) that you were redeemed (ransomed) from the useless (fruitless) way of living inherited by tradition from [your] forefathers, not with corruptible things [such as] silver and gold,
>
> But [you were purchased] with the precious blood of Christ (the Messiah), like that of a [sacrificial] lamb without blemish or spot."
>
> It is true that He was chosen and foreordained (destined and foreknown for it) *before the foundation of the world*, but He was brought out to public view (made manifest) in these *last days* (at the end of the times) *for the sake of you.*

Jesus was chosen and foreordained before the foundation of the Earth to be the sacrificial lamb that would be slain for the sins of the world. The redemptive work that He did was actually planned and put into motion long before God created the heavens and the earth. Through His great sacrifice, there are many things, *immediately available* to us when we confess Jesus as our Lord; other parts of God's plan for our life take time to be released.

Look again at the last part of that passage. It says that Jesus was brought into public view, or made manifest, in these *last days*, for our sake. So although God's plans, purposes, times, and seasons were all thought of and laid out way ahead of time, they are not always brought out into public view right away. They are what I like to call *time-released* events.

Let's take a look at what it means to walk *in* and walk *out* of God's divine plan and learn the importance of aligning our life with His purposes.

CHAPTER I

Blessings That Are Available Immediately

Before we focus our attention on God's time-released plans, I want to make a clear distinction about His plans and purposes that are *not* time-released. These things have already been obtained and have been made available to us through Jesus' shed blood and His finished work on the cross; accessing these things is not dependent on a time or season.

Through our confession of faith in Jesus as our Lord and Savior, there are certain things that are ours. These include healing for our body and wholeness in every area of our life. God's favor and wisdom are also available (Psalm 5:12; James 1:5). As believers, we have the ability to hear God's voice and receive His wisdom to do anything we need to do, from raising our children to ministering in His name.

Non time-released plans and purposes are the things that God actually *downloaded* into our spirits the moment we accepted Jesus into our life. It's as if our internal shelves have been stocked with all the ability we need to overcome the world in every single situation that we will face (Ephesians 1:3). Second Peter 1:3 says,

> His divine power has given us *everything* we need for *life* and **godliness** through our knowledge of him who called us by his own glory and goodness (NIV).

So we have been "loaded up" with everything we need that pertains to life and godliness. This includes all *spiritual* blessings and *natural* blessings. Again, this has already happened. The possibility for us to obtain these things already exists — not somewhere in our future; they are available *now*. As we regularly spend time in the Word of God and prayer, we receive understanding about all that is ours in Christ. Accordingly, these things begin to come to us. All we have to do is reach out and grasp hold of them by faith. Hallelujah!

Paid in Full at the Cross

I really want to iron out this principle for you. There are certain things that are given to you and me by God at salvation. It's like an inheritance that we receive because Jesus died for us — just like a child receives an inheritance through the death of a parent. So, we don't look for these things to come to us in the future. We look to the cross to see what Jesus has already obtained for us through His redemption.

Through His death, burial, and resurrection things like righteousness, peace, and joy have *already been bought* and are ours (Romans 14:17). However, you and I must choose to grasp them. They are not forced on us by God; they are simply made available to us. If we choose not to grab hold of them by faith, they will lay dormant on the inside of our spirit and remain un-manifested in our lives.

We need to be reminded often that Jesus Christ obtained everything we need over two thousand years ago, but we must take hold of it, by *faith*. As we read, study, and meditate on God's Word, our lives are changed. Second Corinthians 3:18 says,

> And all of us, as with unveiled face, [because we] continued to behold [*in the Word of God*] as in a mirror the glory of the Lord, are constantly being *transfigured* into His very own image in ever increasing splendor and from one degree of glory to another; [for this comes] from the Lord [Who is] the Spirit.

While the Lord is the one who transforms us, there is still something we have to do. God doesn't run us down on the road or hold us down and make us take what Jesus paid for. No! We must stay in fellowship with Him and cooperate with the work of His Spirit in our life. Then and only then we can fully grasp what is already ours through Christ.

The truth is, God's life — the life that He offers us through faith — is a *life to be lived!* We are not meant to just accept Christ, die, and go to heaven. We are meant to be people who know about and grasp hold of all the wonderful things that are ours through Jesus *now.* Again, we have been given a *life to be lived.* This is what sets us apart and distinguishes us from all other beings on the face of the Earth.

CHAPTER 2

God's Time-Released Plans

While some of what God has planned and purposed for our life is immediately available, other things, as I said before, are *time-released*. There are certain things that will only come to us over time, in specific seasons. In other words, *they happen as we **go** in God*. For instance, I have some things in my heart that God has talked with me about and I know that they will only be worked out in God's timing. But much like a child, *in my humanness* I want them now — right now! Nevertheless, I need to wait.

The truth is, our life in God, is much like a *journey*, and what we must realize is that where we are today is not where we will remain. We all start somewhere and then we go and go and go and go and go until we reach the end of the journey. However, we don't get to the end of the journey until we have walked, ridden in a car, or done something to be transported. In short, we don't get to the end of the journey until we have gone *the entire way*. There are *no shortcuts* — none!

There are some things in our walk with God that simply do not move up in time. In other words, they do not come to us; we must go to them. As we faithfully serve Him, we will eventually arrive at and live out God's time-released plans and purposes for our lives. It will be in the fullness of *His* time.

Jesus Came in the Fullness of Time

Jesus' life here on Earth is a perfect example of a time-released plan of the Father. Galatians 4:4-5 says,

> But when the *fullness of the time* had come, God sent forth His Son, born of a woman, born under the law, to redeem those who were under the law, that we might receive the adoption as sons (NKJV).

So, we see that although Jesus' life was foreordained before the foundation of the world, He was not manifested until the *fullness of time*. He was not manifested in the first week or the first thousand years of creation. He wasn't even manifest in the first two thousand years. It wasn't until the end of four thousand years of the plans and purposes of God operating, that Jesus came.

The Bible is saying that in the **most perfect time**, Jesus was made manifest and He came forth and was born of a woman. It was also prophesied that He would be crucified on the cross. Actually, the reason for Jesus' birth was His death. However, that didn't happen right after His birth; He lived over thirty-three years. In everything that Jesus did, He walked out what was prophesied about Him in fulfillment of His Father's plan in the Scriptures.

There was a time in the early part of Jesus' ministry when some people tried to kill Him (Luke 4:28-30). While ministering in the synagogue of His home town of Nazareth, many people became very angry with Him because of the things He was saying. Their anger quickly turned to hatred, and they pushed Him out of the city, leading Him to the brow of the hill on which their city was built. They intended to throw Him down and push Him over the edge of the cliff. But the Bible says, "...passing through the midst of them, He went on His way" (Luke 4:30 NKJV). Why did He escape? *It wasn't His time.*

In another situation, one of Jesus' brothers came to Him and said, "Are you going to Jerusalem now?" And He said, "No, *it's not My time yet.*" Jesus, who is the living Word of God in the flesh, knew that Jerusalem was where He was going to go to the cross. He had an amazing sense of God's timing and knew it wasn't time for Him to die; so He declined the appeals to go to Jerusalem.

Jesus was so precisely in tune with the redemptive work of God in and through His life, that every single day was exactly set and fulfilled by Him. God's plans for His life were not determined by the Roman government or the Jewish leaders. He was absolutely on the "clock of God." Actually, all of the feasts that are set on the Jewish calendar are on the clock of God. They were arranged that way from the foundation of the world to coincide with Jesus' life.

Clearly, Jesus' life was on a set track and He couldn't speed it up or slow it down. He simply remained in close fellowship with His Father, and *went to* the events that were laid out for His life, and fulfilled them. In the same way, your life can be set on the clock of God. Regardless of what the government or anybody else says, God's plans and purposes for your life can be set and fulfilled every day. All you need to do is stay close to His heart and *walk them out.*

CHAPTER 3

Zachariah and Elizabeth's Part

Another good example of God's plans and purposes being walked out is seen in the lives of Zachariah and Elizabeth. Let's look at Luke 1 and get a glimpse of the background of their story.

> **In the days when Herod was king of Judea there was a certain priest whose name was Zachariah, of the daily service (the division) of Abia; and his wife was also a descendant of Aaron, and her name was Elizabeth.**
>
> **And they both were righteous in the sight of God, walking blamelessly in all the commandments and requirements of the Lord.**
>
> **But they had no child, for Elizabeth was barren; and both were far advanced in years.**
>
> Luke 1:5-7

Now, we see here in verse 7, as well as in other verses of Luke 1, that Elizabeth and Zachariah's heart's desire was to have a child. What they didn't know, was that it was also a personal desire of God. In fact, God was the one who put the desire in them. Because they were *well advanced in years* (that means really old), it seemed like it would never come to pass. So Elizabeth and Zachariah were living with this unmet, unfulfilled personal desire in their heart.

What they didn't realize was that in a very short time they *would* have a child, and the child they would have would be very special. Who was their child? John the Baptist. He would be the fulfillment of prophecy. He is written about in Malachi, Isaiah and other places in Scripture. Referring to John the Baptist in Malachi 3:1, it says,

> **"Behold, I send My messenger, and he will prepare the way before Me. And the Lord, whom you seek, will suddenly come to His temple, even the Messenger of the covenant, in whom you delight. Behold, He is coming," says the Lord of hosts.**

(NKJV)

And so, this event for Zachariah and Elizabeth was actually planned before the foundation of the earth; and it was that John the Baptist, *their child*, would be the forerunner of Jesus. Consequently, this plan could not be rushed; it could not be pushed up because it needed to fit in the overall collaboration of God's Master plan to send His Son, the Redeemer, to all Mankind. Glory to God!

Are you seeing how the plan of God is unfolding here in Zachariah and Elizabeth's life — even though they were *older*? Now, you might be thinking, *"Do you mean we've got to get older in order to see God's plans and purposes come to pass in our lives?"* Yeah, I believe in many cases we do need to get a little older. God knows the correct time for every part of His plan to be released in our lives, and if it is when we are older, then it's when we're older. We are not going to make it come any sooner.

An Unexpected Visitation

Now, I don't want you to miss some important things about Zachariah and Elizabeth. The Bible says they were *righteous* in the sight of the Lord and they *faithfully followed His commandments* and did what the Lord required of them. In other words, they continued to do the things that they knew to do every day. ***They were faithful to the Lord.*** Let's pick up the story in Luke 1:8-13.

Now while on duty, serving as priest before God in the order of his division, as was the custom of the priesthood, it fell to him by lot to enter [the sanctuary of] the temple of the Lord and burn incense.

And all the throng of the people were praying outside [in the court] at the hour of the incense [burning]. And there appeared to him an angel of the Lord, standing at the right side of the altar of incense.

And when Zachariah saw him, he was troubled, and fear took possession of him. But the angel said to him, Do not be afraid, Zachariah, because your petition was heard, and your wife Elizabeth will bear you a son, and you must call his name John [God is favorable].

So here we see Zachariah was faithfully serving the Lord, going to the temple *every day* and fulfilling the daily duties of his calling. Every now and then he was asked to burn the incense, which was a very high honor. Now, you need to realize that since Zachariah was well advanced in years, some of his duties may have become mundane or gotten kind of old, including burning the incense.

Whatever the case may be, Zachariah continued to faithfully serve the Lord, doing the daily duties of the temple. Once again he was chosen to be the priest to go into the sanctuary and burn the incense. But on this particular day, something was different. This time an angel of the Lord appeared to him with a message from God.

I believe that Zachariah didn't pray for this to happen; and we certainly cannot infer from the Scriptures that He did. He didn't say, "Now Lord, I'm going to burn incense at the temple in two or three days, and I'd really like to see an angel and hear a message from You." No! Zachariah didn't know anything about the events that would take place. It was just part of the plans and purposes of God that started happening before his very eyes. But please realize, it couldn't have happened any sooner than it did.

The angel continued talking to him in verses 14-17 saying,

And you shall have joy and exultant delight, and many will rejoice over his birth, for he will be great and distinguished in the sight of

the Lord. And he must drink no wine nor strong drink, and he will be filled with and controlled by the Holy Spirit even in and from his mother's womb.

And he will turn back and cause to return many of the sons of Israel to the Lord their God, and he will [himself] go before Him in the spirit and power of Elijah, to turn back the hearts of the fathers to the children, and the disobedient and incredulous and unpersuadable to the wisdom of the upright [which is the knowledge and holy love of the will of God] — in order to make ready for the Lord a people [perfectly] prepared [in spirit, adjusted and disposed and placed in the right moral state].

At this point, Zachariah is baffled and responds to the angel, "…By what shall I know and be sure of this? For I am an old man, and my wife is well advanced in years." (Luke 1:18) In other words, Zachariah says, "Hey, look…I'm old. And I'm not an old guy who's married to a young girl. Both of us are old. How can I know for sure that what you're saying is going to happen?"

Now, before we point a finger of judgment at Zachariah for doubting the angel's words, let's stop for a moment and put ourselves in his shoes and think of how we would have responded. We probably would have said something very similar. I wonder what the angel thought of Zachariah's response. Being an eternal being, I wonder if the angel thought, *"Old? Let's see…what does that have to do with the plan of God?"*

Look how the angel answered him:

…I am Gabriel. I stand in the [very] presence of God, and I have been sent to talk to you and to bring you this good news. Now behold, you will be and will continue to be silent and not able to speak till the day when these things take place, because you have not believed what I told you; but my words are of a kind which will be fulfilled in *the appointed and proper time.*

(Luke 1:19-20)

Look again at what the angel said: "But my words are of a kind which will be fulfilled in *the appointed and proper time.*" Wow! That sounds like a time-released event, doesn't it?

Gabriel then goes on to say, "Zachariah, my words are different than yours. You are talking about being old and advanced in years. You are too focused on who you are in the natural, and because of that, I am going to make it so that you are unable to say anything from here on out. There are a lot of things that God has planned that you are just not aware of right now. So the best thing for you to do is keep silent."

What Does This Say to You and Me?

It says that our mouth can get us into a lot of trouble. If the Lord has spoken something to our heart and confirmed it through His Word, but we don't understand it yet, we need to keep our mouth closed. Why? Because we might not experience God's plan if we let our mouth say whatever it wants to say.

The truth is, God has plans and promises for your life — yes, *your very own life*. And they will be fulfilled at the *proper time*. God has plans and promises that connect you with other people. He has plans and promises along with the needed anointing that connect you to His purposes in the earth. There are people, places and anointings that we cannot clearly perceive or know of yet.

So what are we to do? I believe we need to learn to be happy with the things that God *has* given us (1Timothy 6:6). We need to learn to be content with the things we can clearly perceive and *just do them.* The things that seem unclear, hazy or gray, we need to leave alone. If we will just put them on the shelf, so to speak, and begin doing what God has called us to do, we can truly connect with Him. Remember, He is not limited or inhibited by our age, level of education or anything else. Glory to God!

Just as Zachariah and Elizabeth were a part of God's master plan, He also has plans for you and me. These plans are of such great magnitude and purpose in this hour, they will actually take us to the end of our race. However, they have to be fulfilled in the proper and appointed time and won't come before then.

CHAPTER 4

Simeon's Place in History

In Luke 2 we find another man who was walking in accordance with God's divine plans and purposes. His name was Simeon. Like Zachariah and Elizabeth, he was also righteous and faithful and a man upon whom the Spirit of God rested. Let's look at his story.

> Now there was a man in Jerusalem whose name was Simeon, and this man was *righteous* and *devout* [cautiously and carefully observing the divine Law], and looking for the Consolation of Israel; and the Holy Spirit was upon him.
>
> And it had been divinely revealed (communicated) to him by the Holy Spirit that he would not see death before he had seen the Lord's Christ (the Messiah, the Anointed One).
>
> And prompted by the [Holy] Spirit, he came into the temple [enclosure]; and when the parents brought in the little child Jesus to do for Him what was customary according to the Law, [Simeon] took Him up in his arms and praised and thanked God and said, And now, Lord, You are releasing Your servant to depart (leave this world) in peace, according to Your word.
>
> For with my [own] eyes I have seen Your Salvation, which You have ordained and prepared before (in the presence of) all peoples, a Light for revelation to the Gentiles [to disclose what was before

157

unknown] and [to bring] praise and honor and glory to Your people, Israel.

Luke 2:25-32

Wow! Let's just stop and think about this man here. He is old — *very old*. Yet, God at some point earlier in his life gave him an indication by the Holy Spirit that he would not see death before he saw the Savior, the Messiah. Now, Simeon did not see Jesus immediately after the Holy Spirit had revealed this to him. He probably didn't see Him in the next year either. More than likely, it was many years between this revelation from the Holy Spirit and the time Simeon actually saw and held Jesus in the temple.

Again, keep in mind the Scriptures say Simeon was very old. Honestly, when you think about it, this man was like a *living hour glass* — his life was like a *time piece* for God. The Holy Spirit told him that he wouldn't see death until the Savior came to earth and his eyes saw Him. So each day of Simeon's life was like grains of sand slipping through an hour glass. Talk about a *time-released* plan of God! Amazing!

What Did Simeon Do?

We know from what we just read that Simeon sanctified Jesus according to the custom of the Jewish Law and gave Jesus a particular blessing or impartation. There was something that actually had to be transferred from Simeon, *a man of the earth*, into Jesus, *the Son of God*, to help Him with His divinely set course in life. Isn't that remarkable?

We are not told in the Word of God exactly what that impartation was; we know that it was extremely important. So important, that the Holy Spirit told Simeon, "You are not going to leave this earth until *this* is done." Once this task was fulfilled, then he would be released from the Earth.

Think about this; Simeon was ordained by God to be one of the people to publically proclaim the identity of Jesus and impart a blessing on His life. Scriptures say that the Holy Spirit *prompted* him to go to the temple the day Jesus was there.

158

You know God's Spirit prompts us to do things, too. His promptings don't come to us like a big block of concrete falling from above and hitting us on the head. Although that would probably help some of us, God's promptings usually come to us in the form of a gentle nudge on the inside. I wonder how many Christians today totally miss what God has planned and purposed for their life because they have not obeyed His promptings.

Just imagine what would have happened if Simeon would have chosen *not* to go to the temple that day. Wouldn't it have been awful if he would have said, "I've lived all this time and I've never missed going to the temple. So for today, I'm not going to go. It doesn't matter what I do. I'm old and no one cares about me. I just go and sit in the same old seat every week. It really doesn't matter if I'm there." Wow! He would have *totally missed it*! And at the same time, Jesus would have missed out on something too.

So what happened after Simeon blessed Jesus? He turned to Joseph, the child's legal father, and Mary, his mother. As they stood there marveling at what he had just said about Jesus, Simeon began to speak a blessing over Mary saying,

> ...Behold, this Child is appointed and destined for the fall and rising of many in Israel, and for a sign that is spoken against. And a sword will pierce through your own soul also — that the secret thoughts and purposes of many hearts may be brought out and disclosed.
>
> Luke 2:34-35

In addition to standing in the temple and imparting a special blessing to Jesus, God also used Simeon to confirm to Mary what He had spoken to her through the angel Gabriel about a year earlier — that she would give birth to the Savior of the world (Luke 1:26-35). Indeed, Simeon not only prophetically confirmed to them the existence of the Messiah, but also that their baby Jesus *was* the Messiah.

Oh my! Can you see how important this is? How many people do not fully understand or know the true identity of Jesus? Do you realize that many people *do not know* Jesus exists as the Healer, the Transformer of our soul, the Renewer of our mind, the Provider of our needs, and the One who has come to give us wholeness and prosperity? This is the powerful truth that Simeon confirmed to Jesus' parents.

Just as God used Simeon to confirm to Mary and Joseph who Jesus was, He wants to use you and me to confirm to others who Jesus is. There are people everywhere who desperately need a confirmation of who Jesus Christ is. Most of us dress up in our nice clothes and go to church every Sunday and receive a heaping flood of revelation and truth from God. Yet, there are countless people all around us who don't know anything about Jesus or the powerful privilege we have of being born again.

If you are a son or daughter of God and know who Jesus is, I encourage you to be ready to give a reason for the hope that is within you (1 Peter 3:15). As you walk out God's plans and purposes, be ready to **confirm to the world who Jesus is**! It will be required of you!

CHAPTER 5

Align Your Life with God!

We have talked about Simeon, Zachariah and Elizabeth, and Jesus. Each of them walked *in* and walked *out* God's divine plan for their life. They experienced His blessings because ***they aligned their lives with His purpose***. Aligning our lives with God's purpose is the key to experiencing all that God has planned for us.

Now, to align ourselves with God's purpose, we have to be very *watchful and obedient* to His Word. It does not matter what other people are doing or saying, and it does not matter what we personally like or dislike. To align ourselves with the purposes of God in our lives, we have to be very watchful and very obedient to do what God has placed in our hearts to do. We can't just hear about and know the right thing to do; we must actively be doing it! (See James 1:22-25.)

As a result, we can experience the blessings of God flowing in our life *every day*. Every day we can be healed. Every day we can be righteous in the sight of God. Every day we can have wisdom and grace to handle every situation that comes our way, including the job of raising our children. Why can we experience all these blessings and many others? Because of what Jesus gave to us on the cross. Glory to God!

My husband and I have three grown children. They are now thirty-two, thirty-three and thirty-five, which, by the way, is hard for me to believe sometimes. But God gave us wisdom and grace to raise them, and He's still giving us wisdom and grace today. You may not know this, but at times it requires more wisdom and grace to watch your children raise children. We found this to be scary — scarier than some of the things we went through when raising our children. Thank you Jesus for the wisdom to raise my children and grandchildren!

Arriving on Time to Divine Appointments

Like Zachariah, Elizabeth, Simeon and Jesus, there are *divine appointments* awaiting you and me as we walk with God. In order to keep them, we must align our life with His purposes every day. There is a reason for us being here and it is not only to be healed and blessed. There are *divine appointments* for you — specific things for you, and you alone, to walk out before God. They are not for your pastor or for the people on staff at your church. They are for *you!* And when the right time comes, you will know what, where and how to do it.

Life is a lot like a clock. Picture one of those original styled wrist watches — you know, the kind with a round glass face with an hour hand, a minute hand and a second hand. On this kind of watch, the only thing that we can see constantly moving is the second hand. Now if you were to monitor the watch for a few minutes, then you would see the minute hand move slightly every sixty seconds or every time the second had made one complete trip around the clock. Also, if you really had a lot of time on your hands, you could sit and watch the minute hand move around the clock sixty times, and then you would see the big hour hand move.

Is there a point for me saying all that? What does all this mean to you and me? Well, every day of our life is like the movement of the second hand on a watch — it's constantly ticking away, but appears very uneventful. I think we can all identify with this. Its cumulative effects of seconds expiring shall deliver the expiring of minutes — then hours. As the "minute" hand of our life moves around sixty times, the "hour" changes.

God's main events, or divine appointments, are probably not going to take place on the "second" hand of your clock, and seldom are they going to happen on the "minute" hand of your clock. More than likely,

God's divine appointments are going to come to pass, and be marked by your "hour" hand.

Connecting the Dots of Destiny

So what helps us to keep on "ticking" and connects us to the divine appointments of our life? For Zachariah and Elizabeth, Simeon, and many others in Scripture, continuing in the Law of the Lord and walking blamelessly in all His commandments and requirements motivated them and kept them moving forward. In other words, they walked in and were careful to *obey* what they knew in their heart was right. This same principle holds true for us.

Stop for a minute and ask yourself this soul-searching question: *Am I absolutely, positively walking in what I know is right?* This is not for your spouse, your children, or your parents to answer. No! This is for you and you alone. Ask the Holy Spirit to show you anything that you are not doing that He has already prompted you to do. If you are not walking in what you know is right, you are going to miss the divine appointments God has ordained for you along with many other blessings.

You and I cannot fabricate God's divine events or make them come to pass in our own ability and time frame. They are divine. But what we *can* do is walk in obedience to the truth of the Word we know. As we get more light, or understanding of truth from God's Word on who we are in Him, what we have in Him, and what we are to do with what we have, we can learn to be thankful and walk it out. God counts our faithful obedience as an awesome thing!

Along the way, we are to *worship* God. This means to give Him thanks and praise for what He's done in our lives as well as for *who* He is. Yes, we can worship Him at church, but we should also worship Him when we are in our car, at work, on the computer, outside in the yard, or anywhere. I don't mean we have to fall on the floor two or three times a day and bow ourselves to the ground and face a certain direction. No! That's not why God saved us.

God went through a lot of trouble and expense to restore our relationship with Him and came to live in our heart for a purpose.

His deepest desire is to have a **continual connection** with us *all day long, every single day of our lives*!

Just give yourself to God and worship Him. Learn how to be led by His Spirit, doing the things He prompts you to do in the natural as well as the things He prompts you to do in the spirit. This is the *dual life* He has redeemed you to live — one in the natural and one in the spirit. As you "do" the Word and practice being led by God's Spirit, following His peace in your heart, you won't miss His divine appointments. Hallelujah!

CHAPTER 6

Follow the Highway in Your Heart

What God has ordained for you, He has already placed in your *heart*. It's not in your mind — it's in your heart. Let those words sink in. You will not find God's divine plan for your life in your mind; you will only find it in your heart. It might not be very prominent, but it's there. Through the work of the Holy Spirit, He will reveal its details. This is one of the things the Lord has continually impressed on my spirit for the Church of our Lord Jesus Christ for quite some time.

Look at what the Bible says in Psalm 84:5

> **Blessed (happy, fortunate, to be envied) is the man whose strength is in You,** *in whose heart are the highways to Zion.*

In other words, those who trust in the Lord and draw their strength from Him have a highway in their heart that leads to God's purpose and plan for their life. If you are a believer, you have a highway in your heart to follow — a spiritual pathway that was made just for you to travel. This road in your heart has one primary purpose: It is designed by God to take you from where you are to the divine destination He has planned for your life.

What's the Best Way to Follow?

The best way to follow the road is to get on it and move at a steady pace. Don't get lost staring at the scenery, and don't keep looking from side to side trying to see *sparkly* things, like angelic visitations. If you do, you will probably end up running into a ditch. Instead, stay on your designated path at a steady pace, and by all means, don't stop!

Another important thing to remember to help you stay on the highway in your heart is to **not let your mind get bored and wander.** Even though the road that you are on can seem uneventful and mundane, stay on it. Don't be as impatient children traveling in the car who constantly say, "Are we there yet? Are we there yet? I just can't wait! This is taking forever."

Realize that if God wants you on the road you're on, then you have all the strength that you need to stay on it. This road could be a job, a church or a relationship that you want to leave. You may be praying, "Oh, no God! I just can't stay here. Not another dull prayer meeting! Not another boring youth service! No! I'm not going! I can't do this anymore!" But the Lord says, "No. I want you to stay put." Again, if God wants you on a particular path, stay on it! He has a purpose! Listen to these words of wisdom from the Bible:

> **Trust in the Lord with all your heart, and *lean not on your own understanding*; in all your ways acknowledge Him, and He shall direct your paths.**
>
> **Proverbs 3:5-6 NKJV**

In other words, trust where God has you. Trust that this is the best place for you. Stop leaning out the window of your spiritual car wishing you were on another road. Acknowledge Him in all your ways — on all your roads and in all the places He's prepared for you — and He will direct your paths.

So, we need to stay on our course and maintain a steady pace until we reach our goal. This is the principle of the Gospel of Jesus Christ. Hebrews 12:1 says,

> **...Let us strip off and throw aside every encumbrance (unnecessary weight) and that sin which so readily (deftly and cleverly) clings to**

and entangles us, and let us run with patient endurance and steady and active persistence the appointed course of the race that is set before us.

So keep going. Avoid the temptation to take an exit prematurely, hoping to find a more exciting route. Just stay in your car and keep moving forward at a steady pace. You'll make the best time and get the most out of your journey.

The Danger of Detours

The enemy would love nothing more than to get you off course, so he offers you many detours along the way. But taking a detour without God's prompting is a dangerous thing to do. Sometimes detours take us to roads that are still under construction, and other times they turn into a one-lane road that leads us to a dead end. In order to get back on the right path, we have to back up *all the way* to return to our original road.

Very often, when a person decides to take an unplanned exit off the road that God has them on, they become very aggravated and frustrated and end up exiting too fast and causing major problems for those traveling with them as well as those around them. They frequently wreck their lives and the lives of others who are just up ahead or following from behind.

I want you to know that if you are supposed to exit off the road you're on — if you *are* to make a change and begin doing something different — *God* will provide you with *signs* on the road. The Holy Spirit will begin to prompt you miles or days ahead of the exit saying, "I want you to take this exit up ahead." Until then, ***keep doing only what God has told you to do***. Don't try to bring something to pass yourself. Let God do it; let Him bring it to pass in His perfect timing. He makes everything beautiful in *His* timing, not ours (Ecclesiastes 3:11).

Psalm 57:2 says, "I will cry to *God Most High, Who performs on my behalf* and rewards me [Who brings to pass His purposes for me and surely completes them]!" I love this Scripture because it clearly declares *who* performs things and brings them to pass in our lives — *God and God alone*. It is not us, it has never been us, and it never will be us!

167

If you stay on the road where God has placed you, He's not going to let you miss your exit. He will make sure that you have plenty of *signs* ahead of time so that you don't miss the new path He desires to place you on. He will give you plenty of time to gently press on the brakes and slow down.

Has God given you advanced notice that there is a change coming? If not, *keep doing what He has told you to do.* Don't be an accident waiting to happen. If you've gotten off the path He originally placed you on, repent and get back on the road where He put you. Otherwise, you may wreck everything He has worked to develop in your life and the lives of others.

I have one more strong statement: It is the spirit of this world to always want something different. Because things don't look right or seem to be working correctly doesn't mean we are to change them. God has never changed the plan of salvation. It *has been* and *always will be* about Jesus coming to the Earth, dying for our sins and becoming our Savior. For all eternity, His plan remains the same. He's kind of focused isn't He? And if He is focused, we can be focused too.

CHAPTER 7

He Saved the *Fastest* for *Last*

It is not a coincidence or an accident that you are alive and walking the Earth at this point in history. You could have been born centuries ago and walked on the desert sand with Jesus, but you weren't. You are living in these *last days* — brought into the world for such a time as this.

Actually, you have been around for a long time. You may or may not realize it, but you are an **eternal** creature. Just as Jesus lived in eternity, came to Earth and returned to Heaven, you are a child of eternity brought forth from the nurseries of heaven as a spirit.

I picture an angel coming to the throne of God with a person's spirit in his arms. He bows before God and says, "Is this the one? Is this the next one we are going to put flesh on and send to earth?" And God replies, "No. Take that one back. We have to save it for last! That one is for the last days, the end of time."

Think about it. When do the *best* runners run in a relay race? They save the *fastest* ones for *last*. If you are alive during these last days in which we live, you can know with confidence that you were chosen for this time for a great reason. Glory to God!

Temporarily Assigned to Earth

Again, as a son or daughter of the Living God, *you also live in eternity*. Although you are *physically* on the Earth right now, you are *spiritually* seated in heavenly places with Jesus Christ (Ephesians 2:6). You are a stranger, a sojourner, and a *temporary* resident of Earth. Second Corinthians 5:20 says:

> ...We are Christ's ambassadors, God making His appeal as it were through us. We [as Christ's personal representatives] beg you for His sake to lay hold of the divine favor [now offered you] and be reconciled to God.

What is an ambassador? An ambassador is one who is sent from another place to bring the culture of that place into a new place. Normally, we don't see many ambassadors going from America to another country and adapting themselves to the other country's culture. On the contrary, American ambassadors bring American culture to other countries. They teach the people of that country the American ways, values, language, etc. This same principle holds true for us as God's ambassadors.

When your life here on this Earth is complete, you will return to the realm of the eternal. Whether you are born again or not, when you die your spirit is going to come out of your body and go somewhere — either to heaven or to hell. If you have accepted Jesus as your Lord and Savior, guess what? The angels of God are going to come and take you up to your heavenly home. Your Mighty God is building a house for you right now, and He knows everything you want in it. He even knows of things that you will like that you haven't thought of. How? Because He made you and He knows your desires — even those deep desires that you aren't aware of. Isn't that awesome?

Any *Last* Words?

Keep on making God's choices for your life. Let me emphasize that by saying it again. Keep on making *God's choices* for your life, not yours. Aligning your life to God's purpose is all about making God's choices — in your *home*, at *school*, on the *job*, at *church*, *everywhere*. If you don't know God's choice in a situation, just ask Him. All you have to do is say, "Lord, what would You choose for me to do in this situation?" The Bible says in James 1:5…:

> **If any of you is deficient in wisdom, let him ask of the giving God [Who gives] to everyone liberally and ungrudgingly, without reproaching or faultfinding, and it will be given him.**

God promises that as you sincerely ask Him for wisdom, He will sincerely answer your request. He will not leave you "hanging out to dry." Do you think Jesus loved you enough to save you — to be beaten and bruised and go to the cross and do all that He did for you — just to leave you to fend for yourself in these last days? He's not up in heaven saying, "No, I'm not going to help them. Just let them figure it out on their own. If they turn off the road, wreck their lives and die, that's their problem!" No, No, No! God doesn't think that way!

He has a plan and purpose for your life that has been laid out and foreordained before the foundation of the world — a plan and a purpose for you to be His son or His daughter just like Jesus. He has designed for you to live in this hour for His destiny to be fulfilled. And if you don't know that today, I was sent here to tell you. You are the *only* one on Earth that can fulfill God's call on *your* life!

God has invested much in you. There are great and mighty truths and wonders from His Word planted in your heart, and He has given you the power to be His son or daughter (John 1:12). All He asks is that you take His hand and *walk* out His plan. As you align your life with God's purposes every day, He will empower you to walk just as Jesus did until the very end. Hallelujah!

LaVergne, TN USA
15 October 2010
200898LV00002B/2/P